To Patty

Thank you for
being the light
that you are!
~ Melissa

From

BROKEN PIECES

Master to *Peace*

ISBN: 978-1-09838-151-6 (Paperback)

Author: Melissa T. Walker

Printed in the United States

First printing edition 2019.
Second printing edition 2021.

Melissa T. Walker LLC
P.O. Box 155
Woodbridge, VA, 22194-0155

hello@melissatwalker.com
www.melissatwalker.com

From
BROKEN PIECES
Master to *Peace*

For Aiden,
Never allow your past to determine your future
Nor let a temporary situation determine your permanent
destination
Regardless of the obstacles that may come your way
I will always love you Son
~Mom

Disclaimer

I was in a dark place for years. I was deeply bruised and wounded by the pain of my past. Unbeknownst to many, I hid my anxieties, frustrations, fears, embarrassments, hurt, among other emotions within, and did my best to carry on with life, regardless of the many times I contemplated or tried to end it.

The inspiration for this book emerged as I went through countless hours in therapy, through which I realized that the more I wrote about my experiences, the more I was able to understand why I did the things I did, how I could correct them, and how to grow from the situations that hurt me.

The pages that you are about to read may not necessarily show myself or my family in the best light; however, I firmly believe that for situations to change, and for people to heal and grow, we have to speak up about things that cause discomfort and pain.

There is no hate in my heart for the members of my family described in the following pages, and they are well aware of both my book and its intentions.

For far too long, many people have struggled with their pain and allowed it to transform them into people they weren't meant to become.
This book is a "you are not alone" book. Too many people are afraid of speaking up about their afflictions because of the possible ramifications that may follow.

It is time to step out of our comfort zones and embrace our pasts to build stronger futures that will enable the generations after us, to make better choices.

Please note that the names in this book are fictitious to protect the true identities of the individuals.

I pray for peace, growth, strength, and understanding for everyone who reads this book and anyone who has endured similar situations.

Be Blessed.

CONTENTS

BEGINNING...1
In the Beginning, There Was Dad..............................3
.... And We Called Her Mom....................................16

LOST...**23**
Blindly Growing..25
Broken..33
My Way...or Death.......................................40

TRANSITION......................................**55**
New Life, New State...of Mind..............................57
Toe Tag & Body Bag..67
Alone.... With My Struggles...............................81
Rebellion..105
Fatal Destination..121
All Change Isn't Bad...Is It?.............................135

THELIGHT.......................................**165**
Destined to Be Different.................................167
Truth, Trust, and Transparency...........................180
Master Peace..188

LIFE..**201**
The Spiritual Perception of My Life......................203

BEGINNING

CHAPTER 1

In the Beginning, There Was Dad....

IN DECEMBER OF 1959, a baby boy and his twin were brought into the world by a single mother who was very anxious about motherhood. Unfortunately, one of the twins was stillborn. This single mother was heartbroken, as any other mother would be, but there was nothing that she could do to change her fate, and she had to be the best mother she could be, for the sake of her living son. Through difficult hardships, this little boy grew into the man I call my father.

I dreamed of my father as a loving, caring, supportive man, who would part heaven and earth to make sure his baby girl was taken care of. He'd be the first man to love me unconditionally, and I'd be the princess to his kingship. Unfortunately, my father was not always the man I wanted him to be. In reality, he was a short-fused, quick-to-wrath, judgmental, controlling, self-centered, obligated, if-it's-not-gonna-benefit-me-then-I-don't-care kind of guy. I was blinded by what I perceived as love, and I wasn't able to see what true love was until I broke away from the narrow-mindedness that he exposed me to. What I thought was a loving relationship, between father and daughter, was short-lived.

In my younger years, everyone who knew me knew that I was Daddy's Little Girl. He could do no wrong in my eyes. He didn't spoil me, but he was there when I thought he was supposed to be there, and I thought he did and said all the things that a daddy was supposed to do and say to his little princess.

Our relationship faded away not just because of him, but because of things that I had done as well. I was no angel and never professed to be one. I had internal struggles that I had to deal with on a daily basis. I do believe, however, that there comes the point in everyone's life when they decide to do right, not because someone tells them to, but because they've learned from the repetitive mistakes that they've made throughout their lives.

Once, I was told that you can't always blame people for the things they say or do. In many cases, they don't know any better. Many of my father's ways were set in stone because of the tumultuous situation he was brought up in. His mother worked hard doing many odd jobs to provide for her family, especially since she had another set of twins a few years later. She was an anomaly, as it was not, and still isn't, the norm for a woman to have back-to-back twin pregnancies.

With little support, she did her best to make ends meet. Living in a poverty-stricken neighborhood in Kingston, Jamaica, my father, and his siblings grew up wanting much. They dreamed dreams of having a better life and longed for a stable environment for themselves. Unlike the US, the concept of public assistance, food stamps, Medicaid Insurance, and other benefits for families in need, did not, and still does not, exist in Jamaica.

My grandmother loved her children unconditionally, and her love was just as strong as her discipline. My father often recalled an incident when she beat him in his primary school yard, in front of his classmates, teachers, and parents, for cutting school and hanging out with friends at National Heroes Park (a botanical garden in Kingston that houses monuments and is a burial site for many of Jamaica's National

Heroes. It houses the remains of the world-renowned black activist, Marcus Garvey, as well as Jamaica's first Prime Minister, Sir Alexander Bustamante, to name a few).

My father recalled how embarrassed he was that day and how he tried to actively do right by his mother because she embedded fear in him (even though he misbehaved many times after that). When he was conscious of a mischievous deed he committed, he would try his best to stay away from home because he knew his fate. My grandmother's tactics were different. Instead of chasing him around the yard, she'd cook his favorite meal and wait. The aroma would fill the yard causing my father's mouth to water. He weighed the pros and cons heavily. He knew if he didn't get in the house, he would have no dinner, but if he did go in, not only would he get dinner, he'd get a severe whooping. He always got the whooping.

I say all this to say, my grandmother had values that she wanted to instill in her children. She tried to give them what she didn't have growing up. One of her most significant investments in them was sending them to church. Every Sunday, she got them ready and sent them off to Sunday School, giving them the ultimate foundation for true love and success. While that investment started to grow, the lack of a fatherly presence in the home, for love and guidance, became more apparent. My father had that emptiness placed in him from birth, and he began exhibiting hurt, hate, and resentment from early on.

My grandfather, my father's father, wasn't aware of my father and his stillborn twin until a little while after their birth. In fact, the day my father and his twin were born was the day before my grandfather married his wife (my step-grandmother). The truth is that my grandfather did not know about the pregnancy, birth, or mere existence of his children. It was a mutual friend of my grandparents who enlightened my grandfather and his family to the news. As one could imagine, heads rolled. It was said that my step-grandmother was so angry that she said she would have never married my grandfather if she'd known.

Think of it from her perspective. She met a very nice man, they dated for a while, he proposed, she accepted, and they got married. Plans were made to start a family, and by that time, they already lived in the States and settled in New York. So, for her to hear, not only about grandpa's extracurricular activities but his extra responsibilities, she was devastated.

However, through it all, she wanted him to do right by his child. She wanted him to be a man and take responsibility for his actions. After a few years of sending barrels of goodies, they both decided that my father should visit them in the States during the summers when school was out.

They were able to provide him a great life – one better than what he had been living in Jamaica, even if it was temporary. It would give him a chance to bond with his father and get to know the rest of his family. According to family members, my grandmother wouldn't allow my father to be so far away from her. She possibly feared that he would not want to return to Jamaica after being with his father in the States. She was apprehensive about the life he would be exposed to, that it would be better than what she could ever provide, which would ultimately make her unsuccessful at being a good mother. The reasoning behind her strong guard and will to keep close tabs on my father has been debatable. No one ever really knew her true intentions.

After a struggle with breast cancer, my grandmother passed away. My father was roughly 19 years old. 19! A 19-year-old, in most cases, is never ready physically, emotionally, mentally, or even financially to take care of themselves. (Eventually, you will see what happens to me at 19). My father was now stuck, without much support, with his younger brother and sister. He had never been on his own before, and he did not know where to turn. He was probably scared knowing that his mother, his rock, was gone. He was always able to turn to her whether things were good or bad, but now he was stuck. Imagine not being able to see, or ever hear the voice of a loved one that was everything to you. To this day, Mother's Day is one of the hardest days of the year for him. I'm sure he reminisces on all the great times they had together and all the things he wishes he could have done differently.

At that moment in time, he was lost. What would he do? Where would he turn? The only family that he had left, besides his younger siblings, either lived in the countryside of Jamaica or lived in the States. He used that opportunity to reach out to his family in the States, and to his surprise, he was not received with open arms. Not because they didn't want him, but more so because they were not in a position where they could afford to take care of him. In addition to that, his behavior had become questionable over the years. He was known to be extremely rebellious to his mother, and my step-grandmother was not willing to take that chance and have an uncontrollable young adult in her home. It was a chance his family wasn't willing to take. As you can imagine, resentment started bursting through the seams of his soul. He probably thought that his family didn't love him - just like any young person would after experiencing what he did. Likely, he thought he was useless, and to prove his value my father would find a way to show them that he was worth more than what they could have ever bargained for.

He wanted to make a better life for himself, especially since his mother died trying to do that for him and his siblings. She died determined to make the best of her situation. My father was conceived out of wedlock to a man that he had barely known and to a prideful woman who stood in front of her shame as a strong single parent.

My father was conceived out of wedlock to a man that he had barely known and to a prideful woman who stood in front of her shame as a strong single parent.

Would my father's life have been a little easier if he was able to visit his family in the States when initially offered? Probably. Would he have made the same mistakes? Who knows. I firmly believe that it is easy for people to become a product of their environment. The possibility for them to change is likely, but that would only come through hard work, perseverance, and separation.

Things did not go the way my father had hoped.

With his back against the wall, he decided that it was time to make moves on his own. He was already involved in his church heavily, and he spent most of his time perfecting his musical craft on the trumpet. To this day, I cannot hear a horn and not think about my father. It was his signature – his trademark.

After a few years of trying to find his niche, he thought it might be a good time to settle down. Many of his friends were already married and having children. He wasn't getting any younger and, to remain relevant and relatable to the people he surrounded himself with, he had to make a change. This move would be pivotal to show his family that he would be a success, in spite of the bad hand that he was dealt.

The possibility for them to change is likely, but that would only come through hard work, perseverance, and separation.

I believe that my fathers' popularity at church allowed him to be seen by many, and it gave him an advantage in the women department. Back then, and even now, the women always outnumbered the men in the church. The men always had more options when it came to selecting a wife. My father became very close with a woman whom he believed would make a good wife. While I'm not sure how he determined that, it was evident that appearance would make or break his choice.

So, when my grandfather and the rest of the family went to Jamaica sometime in the 1980s, my father had to show them that he was doing pretty well for himself. By then, he had a steady job and showed great hope of living a prosperous life with or without the involvement of his family.

He introduced a beautiful young lady to his family and professed his love for her. She was his fiancé. Pauletta was a very hard working and intelligent woman with a good head on her shoulders. She knew what she wanted from life and was not the type to settle. My father had found himself a keeper, and he was prepared to do whatever he could to make it work. He positioned himself for greatness. His wedding date was set, and everything was going as planned. He was happy. Then came one of the best days of his young life.

My grandfather came from the States to support his son (only son) on his extraordinarily special day. (The rest of his family was unable to make it. It must have been disappointing not being able to have his entire family there). He arrived at the church and sat quietly, waiting for the ceremony to begin. The groomsmen took their place as the royal blue Volvo with the bride pulled up to the church gate.

Slowly, but eagerly, the bridesmaids made their entrance, and the beautiful bride walked down the aisle. When the bride made it halfway down the aisle, she stopped and was serenaded with beautiful music played by my father on his trumpet. This union signified the moment my father had waited for all his life. He was about to marry the love of his life - his Queen. As his tribute ended, the bride proceeded to walk down the aisle, where she met her future husband hand in hand.

The Minister welcomed everyone and began the proceedings. Musical tributes were made, and the marriage license was signed. The Minister blessed the union and gave the groom permission to kiss the bride. He raised her veil and proceeded to present her with a holy kiss. The church erupted in praise and applause. Everyone was ecstatic. The new husband and wife turned to face the congregation, and my grandfather was floored!

He thought the bride looked a little different, but seeing her face clearly, my grandfather realized that the bride was not Pauletta! She was not the woman that my father had introduced the family to. With confusion deep in his heart, my grandfather wished the newlyweds the best of luck and headed back to the

States, where he made the news known to the rest of the family. No one understood my father's angle or what he was trying to prove, but no one said anything. It was a secret that remained hidden, until now.

His actions posed suspicions in my head, and as I looked over my family life, I began making sense of a life filled with dysfunction and nonsense.

With that said, I wondered whatever happened to Pauletta? When did they break up? Why didn't they get married? No one knows for sure. Several perspectives came to mind:

1.   Pauletta probably realized that there was more to my father that he was not willing to own up to and walked away from everything.

2.   My father probably realized that he could not and would not have the kind of control he wanted if he ever got married to a strong-minded woman like Pauletta and ended things with her.

3.   Or it all could have been a fable built to impress his friends and family.

Finding this out as an adult forced me to decipher some hard questions like where, when, and how did he meet my mother? What was the reasoning behind their rushed marriage? What was she bringing to the table that Pauletta wasn't? Was this the beginning of my father's deception? His actions posed suspicions in my head, and as I looked over my family life, I began making sense of a life filled with dysfunction and nonsense.

CHAPTER 2

.... And We Called Her Mom

MY MOTHER WAS born in Kingston, Jamaica to two illustrious and hardworking parents. Her mother, my grandmother, was a homemaker who made it her duty to ensure her family wanted for nothing. She made sure that her two daughters were clothed, fed, and taught to be outstanding women. During the summer, while school was out, my parents would drop me at my grandmother's house while they went to work.

I remember how strict my grandmother was. Coming from a background where she was forced to be mother and father to her younger siblings, she knew how to control a house. She believed that there was a right way and a wrong way to do everything. There was one thing that always drove her crazy—left-handedness. Whenever she saw me writing or eating with my left hand, she would go ballistic and put the pencil or the spoon in my right hand. I think she was a very anal person who may have had a mini compulsion concerning order.

My grandmother provided support for her husband, who worked hard to keep a roof over their heads. Unfortunately, my grandmother was not able to receive the education she had desired but made sure that her children took advantage of every educational opportunity that presented itself. She did not want her children to grow up without the basic skills that it took to operate in the real world. Much of her love and support went hand in hand with the aid of my grandfather.

My grandfather was a hardworking businessman. He regularly traveled to England in his early years to make a better life for himself and his family. I admired his zeal. He built his family home from scratch, made sure his family had a place to rest their heads and kept money coming in so his family would be well taken care of. He was nowhere near wealthy, but he earned the respect of his family because of his accomplishments. He had a laidback personality that forced you to love him. You couldn't be mad at him for too long. He enjoyed playing dominoes and was, overall, a taciturn man.

In 1994, my grandfather lost his battle with bone cancer. I don't remember how long he had cancer, but I do recall where he took his last breath. At 3¾ years old, I can almost remember him fading away. There were days he had the energy to chat with me, other times he would look and smile.

On that fateful day, we all rushed to his house only to be too late. I sat with my mother in the living room on a cot, with our backs against the wall, as the coroners wheeled my grandfather out on a stretcher with a blue tarp covering his body. Not fully grasping the concept of death, I asked my mother where they were going to take him. I got no response. I looked up at my pregnant mother and watched as she raised her glasses to wipe away a single tear that ran down her cheek. At that moment, I realized that she was human. At that moment, I saw love.

As a child, I viewed my mother as a superhero. She was the one who bathed me, clothed me, fed me, played with me, and there was not one moment where I thought that she was tired, or hungry, or hurting. She genuinely wanted her own family to love and nurture, and when she got the opportunity, she did the best she could. My mother is and has always been, an introvert. She kept to herself, stayed out of trouble, and tried to do what was right. That's more than what I can say for myself. She finished high school and got a job as a secretary at said school. She worked there for a few years until she landed a job at the prestigious Kingston Free Zone. The Kingston Free Zone was a government-owned free trade zone in Jamaica. It allowed businesses, both nationally and internationally, to operate without taxation on their imports and exports. Back in the 80s and 90s, this was a trendy place to work, and it offered significant benefits for employees.

One of the best benefits that the company offered was the option to get first pick of the houses in a new neighborhood that was being developed. My mother saw that and used it as an opportunity to build a home for her family. The house she chose was a brand spanking new 2-bedroom house, in a neighborhood that was considered middle class. We moved into that house when I was two months old, and we lived there until we migrated to the United States, when I was 16.

My mother was determined to do well for herself, and that was going to happen whether she was married or not. After having my brother in 1995, she decided to go back to school, and completed her Bachelor of Arts in Business Administration, making her the first person in her family to receive a college degree. With all of that under her belt, she still found time to be a devoted Christian.

My mother was raised in the Baptist church, and in the late 70s or early 80s, she left and became a member of a very prominent Pentecostal church (the church I was raised in). She always had a passion for children and became a Sunday School teacher for 4 and 5-year-old children in our church. She even sang in our church choir as a soprano! She was very involved and devoted to her church. She tried her best to stay grounded in her beliefs, even through the trying times.

She loved being in church. Whenever there was Bible Study, choir rehearsal, prayer meetings, she was there. If they had two services on Sunday, she was there. Her faith in God was strong, but just like anyone else, she had her moments where she questioned Him. She was not as fortunate as many of her fellow church-goers, and her wardrobe was no exception to that struggle. She usually had to wear the same outfit every other week. One Sunday, someone uttered something along the lines of, "Didn't you wear that last week?" She was aware of her situation, but to have someone else point it out was hurtful. She decided that she was not going back to church. That following Sunday, she laid in bed, looking in her closet, convinced that she would never go back to church because she didn't have enough clothes. Then a small voice said to her, "Whom do you serve, God or man?"

Then it hit her! It wasn't about people or what they had to say. It was about her relationship with God. She got up that morning, put on what she had, and went to church, never looking back - ever.

My mother tried her best to instill Christian values in our home. However, my brother and I (with me being the lead troublemaker) would do anything to stay away or not go to church as often as we did. We would hide her car keys, and whenever she got close to finding them, one of us, usually my brother, would distract her while I put the keys in a new hiding spot. Once we knew that she had given up her search, her keys would miraculously reappear! We found that our tactic worked best around Sunday evenings, right around the time we would have to leave for night services. Even then, she never gave up her faith. She loved God and her family, and she just wanted to do what she thought was right in the eyes of God.

Shortly after transitioning to that church, my mother met my father, and she would not give him the attention he wanted. My mother's mother said that he would come by the house from time to time, trying to get my mother's attention. I don't know what was said or done to get her down the aisle, but one thing is for sure, she needed a change of environment. Her younger sister had gotten married, had her first child, and was transitioning to the United States, while she was renting a half of her parents' home. She was in her late 20s and desired a family, and without much hesitation, she decided to get married.

When she announced that she was getting married, most of her family members were in disbelief. They hadn't seen her date anyone and barely knew the guy that she was getting ready to pledge forever to.

My grandfather was entirely against it. That was his daughter, and he wanted what was best for her, but seeing her marry my father was not on his list. Still, she wanted her freedom. So, she decided to stop pushing against my father, and instead join forces with him, to make the best of what life could offer.

I don't know how or when my parents got engaged, or how long they dated, if at all. I know that an announcement was made, invitations were sent, and my mother showed up on her wedding day. There was no rehearsal dinner, and if there was one, she wasn't there. This was supposed to be her new and fresh start. She was determined to make it work at any cost.

My parent's upbringing was by no means easy. Once they settled in their marriage, and begun having kids, things changed quickly, and not always for the best.

LOST

CHAPTER 3

Blindly Growing

I WAS BORN on a cool Wednesday night in Kingston and immediately became the light of my parent's life. I grew up not wanting much. My parents were always in the home and both did what they could to provide for their family. From the outside things looked pleasing. I thought I lived a pretty decent life. Many of my friends thought my family was well off and, even though that was not entirely accurate. My thoughts about my family were innocent.

I was protected from the truth and was left with premature thoughts and beliefs about what I thought the family dynamic should look like. I thought that just like on TV, men were responsible for protecting and providing for their families, and doing basic chores around the house, like taking out the trash, moving furniture when necessary, and killing and removing lizards, insects, and any other bugs that snuck themselves into our home. And on the other hand, I thought women were responsible for cooking, cleaning, taking care of the children, and everything else in-between.

Boy, did I have it all wrong! It's embarrassing to admit that I thought this dynamic was the norm. I've learned that, in any home, there should always be equal partnership. If the wife can't cook because she's taking care of the children, then the husband should be able to help out, and if the trash needs to be taken out, and the husband is still at work, then by all means, the wife should be able to take it out. When I was growing up, sexist views and stereotypical roles were commonplace, but it never felt right to me. I just did what I was told because I was a child.

From a very early age, I realized the importance of effective communication in every relationship. Maybe if my parents were open to effective communication, perhaps their relationship would have turned out differently. Whenever my mother would ask my father for help, his response would be,

"What would you do if I wasn't here?"

There was no teamwork, just sad misguided stereotypes. My mother would help my brother and I with our homework assignments, cook dinner and take care of everything else while my father sat on the couch reading his newspaper - just like the scenarios we saw on TV.

There was one instance where my mother convinced my father to cook Sunday dinner since he wasn't going to church that Sunday. He cooked curried chicken and white rice, and for me, this was a big deal. Before that moment, I had no recollection of my father preparing a meal of this magnitude. We came home from church, and dinner was almost ready. Before we could sit down to eat, I could hear my mother arguing with my father in the kitchen. Apparently, he made the food so spicy that none of us could eat it. My father made it very clear that he would never help again, and that was that. I've never seen him cook in that house again.

I didn't see many occasions where my parents had effective communication and partnership with each other. They argued and fought over many things, with money being their biggest issue. For many years, it was my mother who was the primary breadwinner, holding down the majority of their responsibilities. I honestly believe that this was one of the main reasons that emotional abuse played a significant role in my home.

In society, especially in the Caribbean, it is common for men to feel emasculated if they do not fit society's criteria for masculinity. In many cases, a man was considered tough, strong, hardworking, and after a long day of work, he'd bring home his paycheck, sit back in his favorite recliner with a cold beer, and watch television or read his newspaper until dinner was ready, all while his wife took care of the kids, the house, and the bills. If the woman made more money than the man, out went his ego and in walked his emotions.

Consequently, my father's emotions shaped me into a confused young woman. I considered myself a no-nonsense type of girl, who was quick to speak before really thinking things through. I could never get friends to stick around. I thought I was a great person, but I didn't realize that my mouth was my downfall. I have missed many blessings and forfeited many chances because of my mouth.

At a very young age, my emotions began to shift. Self-esteem issues developed early and ran through my veins profusely. It was a daily struggle that had me questioning everything in my life.

Why am I here?

What is my purpose?
What do people think of me?
Should I even live anymore?
Would I be missed if I died?
Would I have a great turnout to my funeral?
Who would read my eulogy?
Will people remember me after I'm gone?
For how long?

These thoughts continued for years and intensified with more thought-provoking, self-doubting statements like,
Her hair looks better than mine.
She has a lighter complexion than I do.
I'm not as pretty as she is.
The boys don't look at me the way they look at her.
I'm going to slice my wrists and kill myself. I don't belong here.
Or maybe, I should jump from this building.
No one will ever like me.
I'll never be good enough.
I might as well live this life to the fullest. I'm going to Hell anyway.
I'm just a pawn in this sick game of life.

Then, on top of that, there were so many things

that I hated about myself. I hated my nose. I thought it was too big. I hated my teeth (pre-braces). It made me feel uncomfortable to smile. I hated my hair. It was too nappy and not curly like the other girls. I hated my forehead. It was the butt of many hurtful jokes. It was always the first thing I'd get teased about. I was always the "big head girl", and I couldn't do anything to change it. I hated being skinny. People just saw me as a skinny little girl with no curves, no 'assets', and therefore undesirable. I did everything to be seen and to fit in with the cool kids. I even became the punching bag for a group of sick girls whom I would do anything to hang out with. In the end, I was still seen as inferior and unworthy.

I hated that I was not seen as beautiful, at least not through my concave vision. I needed to find a way to be seen. Some people were popular because they could sing, or because they could play an instrument. Others were popular because they hung out with people who had 'talent'. I needed to find my niche. Fitting in just never came easily to me. I was too young to understand, but self-love was not taught to me. I was more concerned about other people's perceptions rather than embracing myself as whom God created me to be. Even though I struggled with these personal issues, there was something that was still special about me.

While in grade school, my teachers realized that I had a knack for writing short stories and poems. I used words that children my age were unfamiliar with. I enjoyed writing – it gave me life. I liked it so much that I was asked to write a poem for Father's Day to present in front of my entire church. I was in third grade, and I vividly remember my third-grade teacher proudly smiling when she reviewed my first draft. After we put our final touches on it, it was time for me to recite the poem to the 2000 plus members of my church. This was the moment I was waiting for. I was going to be loved for this. People will finally understand and accept me.

Then I froze. The fear of rejection crippled me moments before it was my turn to go onstage. My Sunday School teacher saw my uncertainty and had another little girl present on my behalf. I stood outside and heard the little girl begin,

"Fathers are good, kind and dandy,
but some of them are not so handy.
Good Fathers are like precious gems,
and should be treated like real men," she started.

With clenched hands and crossed toes, I waited, and waited, and waited. The little girl finished the poem by saying, "Happy Father's Day," while omitting the fact that the poem was written by me.

The church erupted! They loved the poem. This little girl was getting all the praise for something that I had put my everything into. However, instead of feeling sad or disappointed, all I could think of was, "Maybe if she had said I wrote it, no one would have been as pleased about it."

My parents, especially my mother, were upset that I didn't present the poem. They couldn't understand why I would allow someone else to showcase my hard work. I didn't have a straight answer for them. I never spoke of that poem again, and just like every other uncomfortable situation in my life at that point, I suppressed that memory.

CHAPTER 4

Broken

FROM EARLY ON in life, I was given a great deal of responsibility. The typical 'clean your room' was just the tip of the iceberg in my house. Every weekend, I was responsible for sweeping and mopping the entire house, dusting and polishing the furniture, cleaning the bathrooms, and occasionally raking the leaves in the yard. In my mid-teenage years, when things became tight, I had to add my laundry to that list. That task eventually expanded, and my father's laundry became my responsibility, in exchange for lunch money/allowance.

On Saturday evenings, I'd have to cut, clean, and season a whole chicken (not the pre-cut and cleaned pieces we get in the supermarket today) in preparation for Sunday dinner. Then I had the daily chores of washing the dishes and pots that were left in the sink after a meal was prepared. The worst time to wash dishes was on Sunday evenings. There were always more dishes and pots because that was the day my mother did most of the cooking for the week. It took hours to get that kitchen clean.

Usually, when I'd complete a chore, my work would be heavily scrutinized. If something was out of place, or not clean enough, I'd have to do it over, and I'd better get it right. I remember one particular Sunday afternoon after all my chores were done, the regular inspection commenced. Upon review, I was scolded for leaving a pot in the sink to soak. It had just been used, and the remains of food were stuck to the bottom.

My father deemed the kitchen unclean, proceeded to demean everything that I had done, and began spewing his typical destructive comments. He cornered me in the kitchen and demanded an explanation as to why the pot was left in the sink. I tried explaining, but he only grew angrier. He resembled a food inspector with pen in hand, ready to take notes. The only difference was he began aiming the pen at my eye, while yelling how irresponsible I was. He grew frustrated when the pen wouldn't connect, but that didn't deter him from his goal. He kept trying. I was furious. I had to do something.

Should I block him?

Should I hit back?

Should I speak up?

Should I walk away?

"What are you trying to do? Damage my eyes?" I asked, shocked.

As the heated blood inside him reached its boiling point, his composure slowly began to change, as did his complexion. He was red with rage and yelled,

"So what!"

It was as though my eyes were mere pieces of paper from a binder that could be easily replaced. I was angry, but I didn't know how to say so without infuriating him further. My ego was bruised. There was nothing I could do to please my father - or my family for that matter. They didn't realize how much I craved their love, affection, support, and attention. They were always too busy reprimanding me to notice.

As a youngster, I was very athletic. I was active in track and field and swimming, but nothing was as rewarding as a great game of netball. At first,

I participated in these sports because I liked them. Eventually, it just became a means to impress my parents. It appeared as though it was working, at least for a moment. They were intrigued because I was doing so well in sports. They were especially excited when my track team and I were invited to participate in the annual Miami Classics track meet in Miami, Florida.

It caused great excitement to see school-aged Jamaican children perform overseas. I believe I worked hard, and I wanted to show my school, my friends, and most of all, my parents, that I could excel at something. And excel I did! I placed second in my division for long jump and received tremendous praise from teammates and school officials. My parents, especially my father, finally had something to boast about, and it felt good. However, something still wasn't right. I realized that they were not there for me, supporting me. I'd never seen them at any of my games or events. The most they would do is drop me off and pick me up.

I initially thought that it was because of work obligations, but my younger brother was just as active as I was in sports and they, especially my father, were present for every one of my brother's games. My brother was, and still is, one of the most talented soccer players ever. We all noticed, and we believed, and still believe, that he's destined for greatness. Secretly, I felt that my father only stuck around because he thought my brother would make it professionally, and he wanted to be there to collect his check when the big bucks started rolling in. I tried my best not to let the lack of support from my parents affect me, even though they supported my brother more. I used my disappointment and harnessed it in my athletic craft. I continued to excel until one fateful day.

It was the finals of Jamaica's Prep Champs, an annual track and field meet where schools across the country competed in various track and field events, vying for the championship. The school I attended was known to have great athletes who took their training and growth seriously. We had a set of coaches who were able to impact and reach out to us kids in a way that made us feel like family - like we were valued.

It was my last turn to jump in the long jump finals. I was focused and in tune. I blocked out all the cheers and chants from my supporters when the announcer called my name. Everyone around me disappeared. The lights faded, and a bright spotlight shone on me. I was focused. I was ready to win.

Tilting backward, with most of my weight on my right leg, I sprinted off my mark, aligned my dominant foot with the pivot board, and flew off into the air. The world slowed down. My legs went in a circular motion several times, and I securely planted my toes in the sand and quickly exited the pit. The crowd went wild, and when I looked up, I saw my mother by the sidelines. I was in a state of shock. This leap was probably the best I'd ever jumped, and my mother was there to see it. It was a great feeling. I ran over to her with the intention to say,

"Mommy, did you see that?"

But instead, what came out was,

"Mommy, what are you doing here?"

She coyly responded,

"I just stopped by to drop some things off for your brother."

I sank. No, I was buried. They might as well have dug a hole in the long jump pit, threw me in, and covered me up. I couldn't do it anymore. It didn't matter anymore. My parents didn't see me. That marked the end of my athletic career. All I wanted was support, and my parents couldn't give it to me.

Why was that so difficult to understand?
Why couldn't they see that?
What else could I do to make them see me?
Did I have to yell and scream?
Did I have to hurt myself?
Why didn't they care?

Nothing was ever good enough. It was time for me to find something else that they could appreciate.

I was always known as a little chatterbox. My parents would say that I'd make a great lawyer. So, I thought that diving into my academics would turn things around. I was on the honor roll, the debate team, and I was the Deputy Head Girl (Vice President) for my Prep school. Things were looking up. I got into a great high school, and I intended to make the best of it.

CHAPTER 5

My Way...or Death

IGH SCHOOL WAS a pivotal turning point for me. Instead of embracing the endless opportunities, I decided to give up. I felt that I had arrived and that I was invincible. I spent many times in detention (we called it community service), and I even got to a point where I was almost suspended from school. All of this before I got to the 9th grade (in Jamaica, high school starts in the 7th grade). The guidance counselor knew me very well and probably saw something in me that I didn't see in myself, hence her continuous leniency. I was overly confident and unstoppable. I began slipping away from the things that were right and focused more on stuff with no substance - all to be seen and heard. I craved popularity and acceptance from anyone who was willing to give it.

In my first year of high school, I felt the need to make a name for myself. It was a brand-new environment. No one knew who I was, and I could be seen as either a strong person or a weak link. I needed ammunition that would leave a mark. My name had to be up there with the greats — something to separate me from the rest. I attended an all-girls Catholic high school. What could I possibly get my hands on that would sell? What did all these long skirt-wearing girls lack? I shut off my moral compass and gravitated towards things that a young Christian girl should have known.

I got my hands on one of the most explicit, offensive, derogatory, and repugnant magazines I could find. It was a pornographic magazine with pictures and stories of various sexual encounters that were lewd and expletive-filled and endorsed everything opposite of what a young lady should strive to become. Back then, cell phones were beginning to gain popularity. They didn't have high-resolution cameras or unlimited internet. The concept of Google was picking up and more than anything, a cell phone was considered contraband during school hours. It served little or no purpose for what my magazine had in store.

Bringing literature like this to school, I'm sure, was grounds for expulsion. I wasn't thinking that far ahead. I just needed to be accepted. People in similar situations never thoroughly think things through. We always think of all the possible positive outcomes but fail to see that the light at the end of the tunnel may not be as bright as we think.

The plan was to charge the girls JMD 50 for every 30 minutes they held onto the book. I was going to make money and build friendships, I naïvely thought. It wasn't a lousy hustle at all. Throughout the first half of the day, business was booming. Girls from all over the school caught wind of this mystical magazine, and they had to come to see for themselves. As each class period ended, there would be a line of girls discreetly trailing, waiting for their turn. Things were looking good, money was great! Again, I went to an all-girls school. We didn't see our male counterparts often, and our teenaged hormones were running wildly. I was on fire, with no fear of getting caught! I was making a name for myself. I was the girl on campus.

I've always heard the expression, never mix business with friends/family. There was a friend whom I knew from the 5th grade. We ended up going to the same high school and were placed in almost all the same classes. She wanted to see the book and not pay. I guess she thought that our friendship meant that she was exempt from the rules. I was not having it. Neither was she.

A few days later, my homeroom teachers decided to do a random spot check. Instantly, I knew that was fishy. The spot checks were never that random and were always on a Tuesday or Thursday. If I remember correctly, it was neither. What made it even stranger was that the check was in the afternoon and they started the search from the row that I sat in. I was the fourth student from the front, all the way over in the row furthest to the right. They usually started the search from the left side of the classroom. Yeah! Something was up, and I had little time to figure out what to do with the book.

I brainstormed for a few minutes, and then I gave up. I didn't care anymore. I wasn't thinking about the repercussions. I wasn't thinking period. They finally got to me. The gig was up. They removed all the books from my bag, almost too quickly, and put them back. My classmates all waited with anticipation. They wanted to see what was going to happen, as I would have done if the shoe was on someone else's foot.

But nothing happened, and just like perfect timing on a television show, the bell indicating dismal for the day, rung, and I was free! Or so I thought. With one foot through the door, my homeroom teachers asked me to stay back. I could've bolted, told them I had a prior engagement, but I stayed. Why? I didn't know what to do. I was overwhelmed with adrenaline running through my veins. This was it - my death sentence. I hated myself more at this moment. The self-loathing that filled me was beyond what any 12-year-old should ever feel. Not being able to vent to anyone, destroyed me.

They asked for the magazine, and in one final attempt to make it all disappear, I asked,

"What magazine?"

They made it very clear that they were not in the mood to play any more of my silly, demented games and, again, demanded the magazine. I surrendered the book as though it was held hostage. All that nervousness about being caught was now directed to my fan base.

Would they disappear?
Would they still know my name?
Would they still want to hang out with me?

My teachers briefly looked at the book, gave me a hearty Christian lecture, which meant virtually nothing to me, and dismissed me. Before leaving, I asked them for the magazine back, with the intent to operate a more covert operation. My teachers looked at each other, looked at me, and scoffed. "You're not getting this book back," one teacher said. Anyone in this situation would probably be gripped with fear. I was more concerned about my fan base.

They dismissed me once more, and I'm sure they were bound to discuss this and show their newly claimed contraband to all the teachers in the lounge, and the judgment would begin because I was supposed to be from a Christian home with strong roots in my church. I knew it was only a matter of time before rumors started to spread, or worse, my parents found out. There was no way that my teachers would keep this news from them. It was too big. At that moment, I was worried, but the callousness of my already broken and lonely heart caused me to think about dying - just running in the street and getting struck by a bus. It would probably have been easier to die that way versus by the hands of my father, because inevitably when he found out, he'd kill me.

But then my focus shifted. My blood became cold and dense. I was angry, and that anger quickly turned into revenge. My intuition, which was right, was telling me it was the friend from 5th grade who snitched, and she would have to feel my wrath later. But now, I had to get home and figure out if my parents knew about my side hustle.

⁓

I usually got home after school, earlier than my parents. I could have used that time to concoct a plan to avoid getting into trouble with my parents, but I didn't. I just waited. I did my homework, took a shower, and watched TV, as though nothing significant happened that day. Instead, I contemplated a plan for that so-called friend. A few hours later, my mother came home, and everything seemed normal. I didn't question it.

I knew he knew. The question was, did he know that I knew that he knew?

Later that evening, while we ate dinner, the headlights from my father's car shone brightly in the house, as he slowly turned into the driveway. I listened intently as the car engine turned off. I heard his car door open, then close. I heard his keys jingle as he opened the door. He walked into the house, and I waited for what was to happen next. Strangely, there was nothing eerie about his entrance. Everything seemed typical, but I just knew deep in my heart of hearts that some significant change was on the way. He exchanged pleasantries with everyone, including me, and that was just utterly mind-boggling. I knew how my teachers were. They had my father on speed dial. If I sneezed, he knew! So, I knew he knew. The question was, did he know that I knew that he knew?

I finished my dinner, cleaned up the dishes in the sink and told my parents "good night" as I proceeded to my room.

I guess I'm in the clear. Let me disappear before...

"Where do you think you're going," a cold, gut-wrenching voice called out from behind me.

When I turned around, my father's stare was piercing through my soul, and for the first time that day, I believed that I was going to meet my Maker in Heaven. He told me to have a seat around the dining table and that he'd get back to me shortly. He went to his bedroom, and I could hear him doing his nightly rituals; reading his newspaper, taking a shower, all of which seemed to take an eternity. I was sitting at that dining table, heart pounding, all because I couldn't fathom what waited for me behind those closed bedroom doors. My mother noticed me sitting around the dining table for quite some time and asked,

"Why did your father tell you to stay here? Did you do something?"

I replied, "No."

Just when I was about to give in and go to bed (I thought he had forgotten about me), out comes my father with the magazine in his hand.

PLOP was the sound that the magazine made as it hit the table.

"What is this? Where did you get this from?" asked my father, in one of the sternest voices I've ever heard.

My world was crashing down. I didn't know how to get out of it. In waltzes my mother,

"What's going on?"

"Look at what your daughter had parading around at school." I was usually her daughter when I'd get caught up in mischief, but his daughter when there was something to brag about. My mother looked over at the magazine and briefly glanced at the pages.

"What is this? Where did you get this from?", as though she didn't hear my father ask those exact questions a few seconds earlier.

I could hear the tone in her voice. She was ready to get all spiritual.

"Where is this behavior coming from? We don't operate this way."

My father, who never looked away from me, was still waiting for his answer.

"Melissa, where did you get this book?"

The 'gangsta' that was left in me was not about to go out like a snitch.

"A friend."

"Which friend?"

"A friend."

My father started naming friends, and I refused to respond. I knew how this night was going to end. Why drag someone else in it. It wasn't going to change the outcome of that night. I refused to give up my source, not so much because I didn't want to be a snitch, but more so because of who I got the book from. My father already wasn't too fond of the individual and seeing that he knew the person's parents very well, that would only escalate the matter.

My father knew how to get information out of me. In the past, he raided my room to find a diary where I kept my most intimate (12-year-old) secrets. He flipped my bed, ripped books from my shelf, threw clothes out of my closet, and moved said closet, to find the diary. Talk about persistence!

This situation would prove to be no different. My father would not stop until he got what he wanted.

"Alright, since you're not gonna talk," he said as

he headed back into his bedroom.

"Maybe this will jog your memory." And out he came with his big black belt.

I still wasn't willing to snitch. I was slightly concerned with why he only wanted to know who I got the book from and not why I had it. Let's be real. I could have bought the book myself. He probably thought that someone put me up to it. He was probably in denial because his little girl, who usually made him look like a good father, should not have been exposed, let alone be a ringleader, to things like this. He always knew I was a lot smarter than the average 12-year-old and being sneaky was my forte.

When he realized that I was not moved by his scare tactics, *WHOOP*, straight across the back. Up until that point, my father had never really hit me before (except the time when I was about 4 or 5, and I cut my hair off. He slapped me on my legs). He was always assertive, and his tone was consistent enough to set my brother and I straight.

I looked at him in shock! I couldn't believe that he hit me. *WHOOP! WHOOP! WHOOP!* Right across my back again. He was swift with his left hand. It was the kind of whooping that was so severe that, even though I tried, no air or sound could escape my mouth. When he still couldn't get the response he wanted out of me, he decided to beat me in between each word in his next question.

"So *WHOOP* who *WHOOP* gave *WHOOP* you *WHOOP* the *WHOOP* book *WHOOP, WHOOP*?"

I sang like a canary bird. Yes, I snitched! I was a whistleblower. I thought that by revealing my source, the punishment would be over. HA! Only in my dreams. The beating became more severe. I can't remember exactly what was being said during that period. I was too busy trying not to die. All the while, my mother was standing nearby, listening to my father unleash his wrath on me. She must have thought that I deserved it, especially since "we don't behave like this."

After several minutes of more intense beating, she came over and stopped him. By then, she could see the blood soaking through the back of my shirt. Yes, my back bled, not profusely, but enough that my mother had to treat the wounds. As she cleaned me up, I couldn't help but wonder what could cause a man, a father, to hit their child the way he hit me.

Granted, I believe I deserved to be punished because that type of behavior should not be tolerated, especially from a 12-year-old. The only reason I could think of was that I tainted his image. I made him look bad. He was supposed to be a revered Christian man with Christian values, and I made him look like a joke in front of everyone in my school. Parents are allowed to feel hurt and disappointment when their children misbehave but, in this instance, he only cared about his reputation. He let his pride to consume him. That day, the pain he inflicted made me hate him. I believed his love was distorted. He just loved me because I belonged to him – I was his possession.

When everything calmed down, he forced me to write a letter to the parents of the person who gave me the book (again, another move to disassociate himself with that 'type of behavior'). It was a good letter too. I can't remember what I wrote, but I remember my mother reading it and questioning if I had written it. Apparently, I had a way with words. She was shocked at the elegance in which I wrote the letter and was pleased with my penmanship (at 12 years old, it didn't seem like my mother knew what my handwriting looked like).

As time passed, I expected him to have a sit-down with me to try to figure out what was going on with me, or at least what caused me to travel down that path. It never came. It was evident that he had an image to uphold, and he would destroy anyone who interfered with his façade. My behavior changed dramatically. I completely shut down from the entire world. It was school, church, home. No friends' birthday parties, no sleepovers (not that my parents allowed that anyway).

When I was home, I kept to myself. I was watching TV when no one was around, or I was in my room listening to music and doing schoolwork. After that beat down from my father, I was convinced that my parents didn't love me or care about me. It was always about what other people would think.

I stopped trying to fight back and focused on the future that I wanted. More than anything, I wanted to leave my parents' house, so I reverted to my childhood dream. The plan was that after finishing high school in Jamaica, I would pursue my college education in the States. I couldn't see life in Jamaica beyond high school. I did not research colleges there, nor did I visit any campuses. I had zero interest. I wanted to leave, with or without their approval, and I was going to do it.

TRANSITION

CHAPTER 6

New Life, New State...of Mind

I N THE 1980S, after my father's mother passed away, my grandfather and his wife decided that my father would be provided with better opportunities in the United States, so they began filing migration paperwork. Back then, the process would usually take a few months to a year to complete, but my father had a peculiar situation that required, birth certificate authentication, DNA tests, and testimonies of family members. By the time the U.S. Department of Homeland Security gathered all the information they had needed, my father had been married and had two children.

However, in 2003, things came to an abrupt halt, when my mother announced she was pregnant with her third child, my sister. This new addition would come at the cost to our immigration process, and my mother's family willingly and lovingly decided to help. In no time, the ball was rolling again and, in 2007, after many years of delays, my family and I, sister included, were officially offered permanent resident status in the United States. I had just finished tenth grade, and I didn't mind detouring from my plan and leaving Jamaica earlier than envisioned. As anyone in my shoes could imagine, I was ecstatic. I couldn't wait to start my new life in the Big Apple, New York City, with my mother's family.

I imagined American life would be like everything I'd seen on TV. I envisioned the white picket fence, charming family home with at least two vehicles in the driveway, great jobs for the parents, college scholarships for my siblings and I, living on campus during my college years, and all that other good stuff. I didn't get a heads up about what I was about to walk into, but I was ready. The transition was going to be smooth and quick.

However, my father had other intentions. He had a change of heart about leaving Jamaica. He wanted the opportunity to come and go. While I'm not too sure what or who he was holding on to back in Jamaica, I was sure it wasn't the house that was about to go into foreclosure or the car that he had already lost. And to top it off, he wanted my brother and I to return to Jamaica with him. He wanted me to finish high school and my brother to start his first year of high school. I'm not sure where we were going to live and what he was going to do to provide for us, but this was his plan, and he was sticking to it.

When I packed my bags for New York, I walked through my childhood home one last time. I knew I would never set foot in that house again. It would be the last time I would ever live there. It wasn't because I hated the house; it was one of the most beautiful homes on the block. It held special sentiments. It's where my brother and I were born and raised. It's where we made our first neighborhood friends and had play dates. It was the only place we could identify as home. I loved that place, but I was just ready for the new phase of my life.

I packed all the things that I believed were important to me (mostly shoes) because I was walking into my new life and there was nothing that anyone could say to persuade me otherwise. My father made arrangements to ensure I was registered for the new year of high school and followed through with the necessary paperwork for my brother to begin high school promptly. As soon as we touched down in New York, I started looking into new schools.

Things didn't begin as smoothly as I'd hope though. We arrived in the States right around the time that the recession hit, so getting that dream job, or a job period, proved to be more difficult than one would have anticipated. Without a great job, it was difficult to have that comfortable life. We lived with my mother's family, which provided some form of normalcy as we visited them almost yearly since I was about 6. Almost immediately, my mother jumped into school to get certified in a field of work that she had no experience in.

My father, well, he stayed home and slept all day (on most days anyway). There was the occasional day where he would walk my brother and sister to school, but on most days, my grandmother would be the one making these rounds. I must give credit where credit is due though. My father took the bus with me on the first day of school, to make sure I didn't get lost and that I would make it on time.

Then the seasons began to change. Coming from Jamaica, cold weather was foreign to me. Up until that point, I'd never seen snow. We only came to the States in the summertime when we had break from school, so I was not prepared for this change. The leaves were changing colors, the air was growing brisk, and I was going to school in a black denim jacket, and a pair of black flip-flops from Old Navy. At first, I didn't think the climate change was that bad, but after seeing people in thick sweaters and boots, I knew what I was feeling wasn't normal.

Things were extremely tight, so tight that my first pair of snow boots and winter clothes came from a family friend who attended our church. It just so happened that her daughter, who was a little younger than me, had a lot of clothes that she'd outgrown. So, I received a whole new wardrobe of clothes, and the family friend bought me my first pair of winter boots. I remember wearing some of my new clothes to church that following Sunday, and the family friend's daughter saw what I was wearing. In front of everyone, she started announcing that she had the exact outfit that I was wearing and began scrutinizing it, as though she saw a familiar distinctive mark that could trace it back to her. I knew she meant nothing by it because she didn't even know that her mother had done this great act of kindness, but I wasn't comfortable with this way of life. My parents were too busy focusing on getting themselves together, and getting rid of each other, that I didn't think they noticed what my brother and I were going through. So, I did what I thought I had to do; I got a job.

My first job was not anything illustrious or worth bragging about. It was your typical 16-year-old's first job—at McDonald's. I hated everything about that job, but it gave me pocket money that aided me the necessary clothing items for the winter. Before that job, I had to start wearing an XL sweater that was previously worn by my father, as a means to keep me warm. The kids at school would make fun of my big sweater, and I was so jealous of all the North Face gear that everyone else was wearing. My job wasn't paying me enough to get jackets from The North Face, but it was enough to get me out of that big sweater. I had to find a way to get away from all the turmoil I was now experiencing. This was not what I thought living in the States would be like.

To make matters worse, things were not getting any better at home. Unbeknownst to many, my parents had a very tumultuous relationship. They'd argue and fight about any and everything. They did not mind airing their dirty laundry in front of their three children, and we knew better than ever repeating anything we saw or heard. I believe that my father married my mother because of her appearance. She is a beautiful woman with long curly hair, chocolate skin, and a beautiful smile. In my opinion, she stood out from most of the other women who they went to church with. It was natural for my father to be attracted to one of the most beautiful women in the church. So, what happened next was inevitable.

After countless counseling sessions with my aunt and uncle, it was clear that my parent's relationship was officially over. It had been on the rocks for years. It was so unstable that I remember my father sleeping on the couch for several years before we moved to the States. My father had to move. The night he left, I remember hugging him and saying goodbye. He seemed to be disappointed that he wouldn't be around his kids. He even got me a prepaid cell phone so that I could keep in contact with him.

After closing the door behind him, I went to the dining room, sat around the table, and tried to eat what was left of my dinner. My cousin asked,

"Are you ok? I'd be going crazy if it was my dad that left".

I brushed it off, assuring her that I was ok, but deep down, I had mixed emotions. I had never lived without both parents. Yeah, they had their moments, but we were always together.

After living without my father for a few weeks, I found myself gradually spending more time at his place. It was a small one-bedroom basement apartment. I converted the living room area into my little space. I started spending weekends there, then weekends turned into weekdays, and before I realized it, I was living with my father full-time. As time slowly passed, his behavior towards me changed. I was starting to understand why my mother wanted to go her separate way. I remember, at one point, he wasn't working for an extended period, and I would go to school, then to work, come home, and he'd ask me what I was planning to cook for dinner.

Back then, I was heavily involved in my church. I was a part of the choir, the chorale, and Praise Dancing. I would often go to Monday Night Youth Prayer Meetings, some Wednesday Night Bible Study sessions, and Friday Night Youth Service. I lived at church. One Saturday morning, I overslept and was in a rush to get to Praise Dancing rehearsal. My father came to me while I was rushing to get ready, to let me know that I couldn't leave until I did my chores. I quickly tried to explain to him that I was running late and that I'd do it once I came home later that day. He grew furious.

He believed that when I returned later that day, I'd be too exhausted, and he wanted the house cleaned before I left. I was persistent that I had to go to church that morning. I called the director, telling her that I was still coming and apologized for being late. We chatted for a minute, and when I headed toward the door, there he was, sitting in a chair to block my exit. He wanted to make sure I cleaned the house before I went anywhere. I was livid! He was taking things far by downplaying the zeal I had about my roles at church. An argument ensued, all while the director of the Praise Dancing Team was on the phone. She heard the things that I said and the things that were said to me. She tried to calm me down, and when the air seemed less tense, she asked me to stay home, to prevent anyone from getting hurt.

When he saw that I was no longer going, he put the chair back around the dining table and muttered under his breath while he walked back to his room. I hated that he tried to control every aspect of my life. I felt that he didn't have grounds to try to control me. He didn't contribute to my education, barely contributed at home, and spent far too much time chatting with random women on the phone about his likes and dislikes.

Things were always getting heated between us, and I felt that eventually, tempers would flare, and emotions would overflow. I believe I possess a sixth sense that allows me to see how some situations unfold, and in almost an instant, the things that were once unforeseen came to fruition. These visions thrust me into a new world, were one of us would probably end up with a toe tag and a body bag.

CHAPTER 7

Toe Tag & Body Bag

I WAS 19 years old and lived in the basement apartment with my father and my brother. (Just like me, my brother had transitioned out of my aunt's home, where my mother lived). During much of this time, I was manipulated and misguided, and often wondered why things in my life were so bad. I witnessed disagreements between the landlord and my father because rent was unpaid for almost a year! I'm not too sure what was happening with my father during this time, but from my perspective, it seemed like he was looking for a handout to make his next move.

One Sunday afternoon, while on our way home from church, he started to complain about a friend whom he had asked for financial assistance. The friend was unable to help him, which made my father irate. The friend had a family - a wife and two beautiful daughters. The youngest daughter had recently graduated from college and was surprised with a car for all her hard work. My father couldn't understand why, in the name of all things holy, his friend would buy his daughter a new car, but couldn't help him financially.

I sat in the passenger's seat and looked at him in disbelief as he continued to ramble about all the "injustices in the world". I couldn't take it anymore. I had to say something.

"That's his daughter, his responsibility, his world. He owes her everything. If he wanted to buy her a mansion or take out a second mortgage on his home for her to go to graduate school, he could! That's his daughter! He owes you nothing!"

No response.

I could not understand why he felt that everyone was supposed to bow down to him. I didn't consider my father a good friend. He would only stick around when he needed you, and once my father got what he wanted, he was gone. He suddenly became too busy to even speak to you. If he was like that with friends, there is no reason why he wouldn't do that with me. He knew that I had a job, and he was quite proud of that accomplishment, but between bus strikes, inclement weather, and everything else in-between, he would never leave the house to pick me up whenever I asked. It wasn't like he was busy. He only came to pick me up once, at a bus stop, and that was in exchange for me buying dinner for the family that night.

Coming home, every night, to that mentality made me want to stay out later and later every night. There were times that I would delay leaving work when scheduled, just because I didn't want to deal with him when I got home. My boss would often force me to go, citing labor laws for student workers.

I felt like I took the place of my mother.

On the nights when I'd get home to unprepared dinner, I felt stressed. If I had been home most, or all, of the day, it would behoove me to have dinner prepared. I'm not sure if that is an old-school Caribbean mentality, where the women (wife, mother, girl child) were responsible for making sure that the men (husband, father, boy child) had all their needs met. It was draining. Anyone who has to do it knows that working, going to school, and then coming home to take care of a family is beyond strenuous. I felt like I took the place of my mother.

With this schedule, it was hard to include much time for my social life and my studies. I launched into a phase of depression, and unbeknownst to me, I started exhibiting the symptoms. The school I attended at the time afforded me with a laptop computer. I turned around and bought another laptop computer, in addition to the desktop computer that was already at home. I didn't need it. I used the excuse that the desktop computer had too many viruses to function normally, and the school computer was strictly for school.

A friend of mine, Cheyanne, gave me a television to take with me to college, and it came in handy. After only living on campus for a year, I brought it back home with me. The TV worked just fine; granted, it was an older model, but there were no flaws. However, I still felt the need to turn around and buy a flat screen TV. The excuse for this large purchase was that I wanted to treat myself for all the hardship that I was enduring.

The frivolous spending didn't end there. Sometime that year, the iPhone 4 was released, and I had to have it. I already had a relatively new phone that worked just fine, but I became so materialistic that I felt I needed to have everything that was new and relevant to feel whole and successful. So, I bought it. My compulsive spending was a silent cry for help.

The day I bought the phone, I called my father to share my good news. He always liked new technology, and I believed that this was a way for us to bond. He was ecstatic. He couldn't wait for me to get home, so he could see what the big buzz was about this phone.

When he saw it, he fell in love with it. After much discussion about what the phone capabilities, he asked if I could buy him an iPhone, and that I didn't have to worry because he'd pay the bill. In my mind, I thought if he could pay the bill, why couldn't he buy the phone? Back then, to get the phone, it was roughly around USD 100, and the monthly bill to maintain the phone was around the same price, give or take a few dollars. Of course, I said no. I wasn't brave enough to say what I was thinking out loud. I knew the type of man he was, and I had to be very careful with my choice of words to prevent any form of confrontation. I was surprised that I said that much. That's when it all started.

The envy that came after was the worst that I'd ever seen. If I had the phone charging on my iHome dock, my father would become engulfed in rage whenever he walked by it. A switch flipped in his head. He transformed into a hateful beast. He had to find a way to gain control, so he created new rules. Effective a few nights after I got the phone, I was not allowed to use it in the house. If I had to make a call or send a message, I had to go outside.

Remember, I was 19 years old, going to work and school FULL-TIME. I was trying to take care of myself, especially since it was hard for my parents to help. I was ok with getting everything I needed for myself, by myself. Out of the kindness and sincerity of my heart, I suggested taking a semester off and working full-time to help out the family, but that was quickly frowned upon by my father.

One night, I was outside on my phone with a friend from Jamaica, Mike (we'll get into details about him later), and we were talking for about an hour or so before we said our goodbyes. I got up, walked through the door, locked it behind me, then gunshots began raining profusely. Being exposed to this act of unfamiliar violence was new to me. The shots rang loudly and sounded like they were only a few feet away, but they seemed all too familiar for my father. He gathered my brother and I and told us to hit the floor. We had no clue what was happening outside, and while our faces were plastered against the carpet, all I could think about was me being outside for just a minute longer.

After what seemed like a few minutes of shots

flying over our heads, things cooled down, and we proceeded with our lives. My father used that as a teachable moment to tell me that I could've gotten caught up in the crossfire if I had decided to stay on my phone any longer. I knew he was right, but I believed that the only reason I was outside, to begin with, was because of his jealousy over my cell phone. He asked,

"Do you see what could have happened to you because you don't listen?"
In other words,

I was his child, but I was no longer a child.

"If you had bought me that phone, you would not have almost been shot."

That's the day I put my foot down. I was his child, but I was no longer a child. I was nothing but productive in school, work, and even at home. My respect for him began to diminish. He wasn't appreciative or respectful of my hard work, especially considering his circumstance. It was time for a change.

A couple of days after the shootout, I was on my phone with a friend in the house, and of course, my father was not happy about it. He proceeded to make a scene about me using my phone in his house, and I was not willing to comply with him. He felt that I was acting tough because I wanted to show whomever I was on the phone with that I was in control of the house. I turned away from him, to minimize what my friend could hear on the other side. I tried to continue my conversation and ignore the irrational voice behind me screaming.

My father did not like that. He began to boil with rage. He stormed over to me and tried to grab the phone away. I gained control of the phone quickly. I guarded that phone with my life because I knew his intentions, and if he had his way, he would destroy it. It was not ok for him to wreck what he couldn't have. I would not tolerate it. It was one of the most valuable items that I owned, third to the computer and flat screen. He continued to rant about me showing off with the things that I purchased, and when that didn't give him the reaction he wanted out of me, without warning, this man, this being, this pathetic excuse of a father, began to punch me in the face.

Yes, punch, not a slap, not a little beating, a grown man punch. Floyd Mayweather Jr. probably couldn't have done it any better. Left, right, left, right. Each blow was worse than the one before. He intended to knock me out cold. He wanted me to become submissive to his ways, and he'd get me to conform in any way he could. He was dripping with envy, hatred, and embarrassment because the things I did for myself, he couldn't do for himself. He was angry about the opportunities that the U.S. had afforded me, instead of being proud of my accomplishments. I've heard him express how much better his life would have been if he came to the States in his youth. All his pent-up anger and frustration about his less than perfect life, he took out on me, and he thought that he was right.

My father used this tactic to try to regain the power, respect, and authority that he lost when he decided that treating me like a wife, and not a child, was the only way he could feel like a man.

Many parents always want to show that they are in control by inflicting pain, hurt, and or humiliation. My father used this tactic to try to regain the power, respect, and authority that he lost when he decided that treating me like a wife, and not a child, was the only way he could feel like a man.

I grabbed my phone and told him I was going to call the police. He made it clear that if the police came to the house that night, he was going to kill me. I hit the call button. The dispatcher asked if he was armed, and I told her that he was in the kitchen, which had knives, and I wasn't sure about what he would do. He was remarkably calm at this point, but I knew he was boiling mad, and I didn't care. Enough was enough.

The operator stayed on the line with me that night, and I'll forever be grateful to her because the anger that was boiling in me was unlike any other.

That night, I wanted to kill my father. I *I* needed him dead. Not just because he beat me up over a phone, but because of how *needed* irrational, manipulative, and controlling he *him* had been over the years. I was fed up. Killing *dead.* him would do the world a favor. Hate was an understatement. I don't even think there is a word to describe how far gone my mind was. Then there was a knock on the door.

My father opened the door, foolishly with one arm behind his back. In front of him stood a police officer. A part of me froze because approaching a police officer with hands concealed usually doesn't end well. With the various acts of police brutality at that time, this incident could have escalated quickly. Even in that mess, God was protecting us both from what could have been an untimely end. Instantly, the policeman, arm on his rifle, politely asked my father to remove his hand from behind him. He quickly complied.

It sounded like the policeman came with backup. I could hear footsteps coming towards the door, and I heard the operator coming over one of their radios.

The policeman stepped into the house and behind him were five more officers! I believed that someone was going to jail tonight, and it wasn't going to be me. They all came in and evaluated the premises; somewhat thoroughly. They checked on my brother, who was in what seemed like a comatose state after coming home late that night. One officer asked if he was ok and if he heard or saw our altercation. I replied,

"No."

A stunned officer chuckled and said,

"He slept through all of this?"

My family was used to my brother's sleeping pattern. He'd get up early in the mornings for school, go to soccer practice after school, sometimes catch up with friends, and once he got home, ate dinner, took a shower, and did his homework, he was of no use to anyone. We jokingly told him that if we were ever to get robbed, they'd clean the entire house out and he wouldn't hear a thing. Every altercation I've ever had with my father, my brother was always asleep. I couldn't help but notice that weird coincidence.

The officers asked us both what happened; I spoke my peace, and so did he. They evaluated my face, and at the time, there were no physical signs of abuse. There was no other form of evidence to prove that we had an altercation, so the police could not do anything. I realized the following day that not only could I visibly see black marks around my eyes, but I also couldn't eat. My top row and bottom row of teeth could not connect. I sought medical attention at a local hospital to correct that.

I felt like my parents had let me down enough for a lifetime.

In a desperate attempt to have him hauled away, I told them about his threats of killing me. I thought that would have been the icing on the cake. Instead, they tried to make arrangements for me to spend the night with my mother. I called my mother – no answer. I called again, nothing. I was running out of time. The officers looked like they were ready to go, and I didn't want to spend the night there. He was going to kill me. I could feel it. When I finally got in contact with my mother and explained my situation to her, she told me that I couldn't stay with her.

I was stunned.

How could my mother, the woman who gave me life, turn me away?
Was I that bad of a person that my mother didn't want

me?

When I asked her why her response was,

"If you called the cops on your father, what will you do to me?"

I'm not sure why this surprised me. I felt like my parents had let me down enough for a lifetime.

Why did I feel so neglected; so unloved?

I felt like my luck was running out, and no one was there to rescue me. After all, if my parents didn't care, who else would?

I resented - no, hated my parents. Real hate, the same kind of hate that someone could have for the devil. I hated them with a perfect hatred. They were beyond the scum of the earth. I didn't want to see or hear from either of them for the rest of my life. I could have cared less if they were sick or dying. I used to coldly say,

I hated them with perfect hatred.

"If they dropped dead in front of me, I'd step right over them and carry on with my life."

I wanted to ex-communicate them. I wished that I could get rid of my last name and disappear from their existence. I was done. Someone did die that night, and it was me - the old me.

CHAPTER 8

Alone.... With My Struggles

MAKING THE ULTIMATE decision to walk away from my family was the hardest decision I had made at that point in my life. It was clear that neither of my parents were in my corner. I had other family members who lived nearby, but I felt that they had done enough for my family. I did not want to burden them with my problems. It was time to pull up my socks and prepare myself for what this ole' cruel world had to offer. I was walking blindly within the walls of what seemed like home, and now I'd be blindly walking through a place where no one cared if I lived or died; if I succeeded or failed; if I ate or bathed.

I ended up staying with a family friend, Harriet, who took me in as her own. I was beyond broken. Getting lost in my thoughts began destroying me. I dropped out of college, quit my job, and gave up on God. I was ready to die; I needed death. I prayed for it and cried about it. I wanted to die in my sleep, and when I kept waking up every day, I was tempted to jump from the top of a building or a bridge. That's the only way I thought I would find peace. It would be my only way to get away from all this hurt and neglect.

The first time I thought about hurting myself was as a child back in Jamaica. I would discreetly cut myself with the intention to bleed out; but my incisions were never deep enough. No one knew. No one saw any bruises or marks. I didn't want to get caught and have people pity me. I just wanted to disappear. I frequently fantasized about my funeral.

Would I have a large turnout?
Would people remember me for the good I'd done?
Did I even do any good?
Would it just be my immediate family?
Who would read my eulogy?
Which pictures would they use for my program?

I would look over my life and try to figure out my

greatest feat and hoped that they would sing praises for the good I did.

Who would throw themselves on my casket?
Who would declare their unwavering love for me?
Would God give me a pass – a restart button to live life all over again under different circumstances?

My thoughts were often in dark places, and no matter how hard I tried, my mindset would not change. My circumstances oppressed me. Harriet, who became a second mother to me, noticed the dark cloud that shadowed me. My lethargic behavior was not something she expected from me. I was usually a vibrant person. My demeanor didn't scare her or make her fear for my or her safety. She was, and still is, a praying woman who would often be on her knees praying to the Lord before the sun would rise.

She and her children prayed fervently for me one night, and almost instantly, I felt like a weight lifted. I tried to get back into the swing of things. I decided not to go back to the university where I started my college education, not because I didn't like it, but because I couldn't afford it. I punished myself for a long time about that decision because it was one of the best schools I ever attended. I applied to a city school, got in, and didn't go to school. I just wasn't ready. Instead, I applied for and got my first job in a bank, and even though it was going okay, it wasn't the greatest. I thought I was ready to be "normal" again, but I couldn't do it. That cloud of doubt was still trailing me.

No matter how often I went to church, or how many different churches I went to, or how long and hard I prayed and fasted, or how much I surrounded myself with positive people, I couldn't shake my depression. The church wasn't encouraging me to speak to a professional. Instead, I was told to pray about it, and God will do the rest. And to add insult to injury, when I did take a step out on faith and spoke to a leader in the church, I'd hear my business from someone else.

I was getting exhausted. I was losing my grip, and after a while, I just gave up – completely!
God didn't care, I thought. He saw me struggling, and He didn't help me.

How could He say He loves me and allow me to fight a losing battle?

I was mad at God. He was on my list - right up there with my parents.

Once I gave it all up, I noticed something significant. Life was like a breeze, and everything felt peaceful. However, the blessings that once followed me stopped! Almost completely. I began failing in my job, friendships were dwindling, and the little love I had left for myself was deteriorating rapidly.

I started going out and staying out late. I'd come home the next day, and do it all over again, without remorse or fear. I was too busy living it up with people whom I thought were friends, getting high and wasted because it made me feel invincible. It eventually consumed me. I thought I was in control, but I was wrong. I didn't realize that sin ALWAYS takes you deeper and further than you expect. Its purpose is to destroy your core and leave you as an empty zombie-like shell, wandering the Earth and causing confusion.

Sin always takes you deeper and further than you expect. Its purpose is to destroy your core and leave you as an empty zombie-like shell, wandering the Earth and causing confusion.

Harriet tried to reason with me. She tried to understand what I was going through and allowed and tolerated my slackness for a long time. I began to take her kindness for weakness, until that fateful early morning when I came home only to be denied access. I rang the doorbell and knocked on the windows. She had had enough, but I was not bothered. I spent my time walking up and down Rockaway Parkway in Brooklyn and jumping into the McDonalds by the L train to grab a bite and use the facilities. I remember, around 4 a.m. one morning, I was sitting on a ledge outside my house with an umbrella over my head as the rain poured, all while still dressed in my work uniform from the day before.

Moreover, the icing on the cake was that I had to be at work at 8 a.m.! An alarm went off in my head, and the trance broke. The tough love that she was giving me started to work. My calloused heart was beginning to shed. I realized that I didn't care about anyone except myself. It was always about pleasing me. I was able to see many of the traits of my father, in me. I had to start over, and I couldn't mess it up.

During my process of regrowth, I fell many times. One night, in particular, I came home late, not as late as when I was living a crazy life, but late enough to spark concern with Harriet. As soon as I walked through the door, her cold, cryptic voice, crept up from the couch,

"You've started with the foolishness again?"
The hairs on the back of my neck stood at attention. Immediately I felt guilty. I believed that I betrayed the trust that Harriet was beginning to regain in me.

I had to do better. So, I got back to my roots. I started going back to church, praying, maintaining positive friendships, and guess what? The black cloud called depression came back; not that it was ever entirely gone, but it came back with a vengeance as if to say,

"How dare you go back to God? Did you forget that you hate Him just as much as you hate your parents?"

All the dark thoughts started flooding my mind once again — thoughts about things that happened to me as a child began to consume me. I was encouraged to go to therapy. I needed help because the memories that were suppressed were now resurfacing with not only the intent to break me but to destroy me.

One of the first memories that came to mind took me back to when I was about 6 or 7 years old in Jamaica. My parents, especially my mother, were very fond of my cousins coming to church with us. These cousins were my first friends, and I looked forward to spending as much time as I could with them. So, every weekend, mostly Saturday nights, my cousins would come over, spend the night, go to church with us on Sunday, and go back home after church. I loved every minute of it. I remember my younger cousin not coming as often because she was practically still a baby and probably required more attention than what could be provided. That's just my guess. I could be wrong.

Every Sunday morning, my mother would start breakfast, then she'd come and wake us up to get ready for church. This task was probably pure hell for her, because it was never easy to wake us up, especially me. I loved my bed, and I still do! She would usually yell and scream before we would attempt to roll out of bed. It wouldn't be normal if she didn't yell. Over the years, my brother and I would secretly laugh or mimic our mother's behavior. She was an interesting character. Hearing her yell at us was like our snooze button. We would roll over and draw a couple more zzzz's.

But, the moment the house became extremely quiet was when we would have to worry the most. She would quietly sneak into our room and start slapping skin left and right. It was either with her hand, a belt, or her infamous slipper. Whenever it got that bad, we knew that we had to get up. You would think that after dealing with that once, we'd learn. Nope! Not us. We did the same thing almost every week.

One particular Sunday morning stood out to me more than any other. This Sunday morning, I didn't hear my mother doing her usual shuffle in the kitchen. She hadn't come to our room yet, and the threat of her slipper was far from my mind. It was strange. The sun was already up, so I knew it wasn't too early.

Did she oversleep?

Possibly. In those situations, I never try to wake her. That would be my free pass to spend the whole day playing! But something else was off.

Why am I up?

I tried to go back to sleep, but then a strange feeling came over me. It was one that I had never felt before and didn't think I was supposed to feel. It was beneath the sheets. I slowly moved the sheets back to see what was there. It was my cousin who was lurking under the sheets, with his hand in my underwear, fondling my private area. I looked at him confused, and he stopped touching me. I looked away, and he began touching me again. This time the touch was more intense, vigorous, and invasive. He was becoming very comfortable putting his finger inside me. There was nothing pleasurable about this

The 28-year-old me wishes I had punched him in the face, but the little 6-year-old me couldn't even utter a word.

unwanted attention. After a minute or two later, he felt he had enough and slipped his hand from out of my underwear, rolled over as if nothing happened, and pretended to be asleep. The 28-year-old me wishes I had punched him in the face, but the little 6-year-old me couldn't even utter a word. I didn't know what to do.

Should I scream?
Should I hit him?
Is this normal?
Am I supposed to like it?
Am I supposed to hate it?

I was solid confusion personified. It was the norm for my cousin to share my bed. My parents probably thought that there was nothing inappropriate about it and, at that time, we were innocent so nothing would happen. They were very vocal about anyone touching me inappropriately and made it very clear that I should let them know immediately if anyone ever crossed that line.

But this was different, right?

He was my cousin, and there was no way that I

could ever tell anyone! I couldn't risk losing my only friend. Besides, my family would think I was lying. I had to make an executive decision, before I even learned long division, that I would not say anything to anyone – ever. The fear of being hated in my family, or treated differently, overtook me.

If I wanted to be normal, I had to exude an air of normalcy, and that molestation was not normal. So, I pushed it to the back of my mind. When I went to therapy to seek help about these thoughts, my therapist explained my experiences as repressed memories. A repressed memory is a memory that has been unconsciously obstructed because of its association with a very traumatic or stressful experience.

If I wanted to be normal, I had to exude an air of normalcy, and that molestation was not normal.

Once that memory resurfaced, I felt even more worthless and insignificant. I remember all the thoughts that ran through my mind in the days and weeks after that incident. I felt that because he touched me, we'd have to get married. I didn't want to be forced into a marriage at 6! I hadn't seen any other 6- or 7-year-olds getting married.

Was I that unique that I'd be the first?
How could I outrun the peer ridicule I'd face as a child bride?
Am I going to hell for not waiting?
Was I in the wrong?
What could I have done to change the outcome of that situation?
Will my parents believe me?
Would they be upset at my aunt and uncle?
Would this cause a rift in my family?

I couldn't afford to lose my family! It was already extremely small. I wasn't sure if I wanted to risk it all. Besides, I figured that it was my fault. If I had gotten up early for church that morning, maybe it never would have happened.

After weeks of trying to figure out my fate, I decided that I had to be brave and bold and speak up about what happened. My friends at school probably wouldn't understand. Instead, I'd be the subject of everyone's gossip. My teachers probably wouldn't understand either, so I asked my mother. Ironically, it was on a Sunday morning. We were parked in front of my cousin's house, waiting for him to get in the car so we could head to church. I'm not sure why he didn't stay with us that weekend, and I didn't ask. I needed to get this weight off my chest before he got in the car. I needed to know what was going to happen to me, without him knowing. This was it.

I opened my mouth, but no words came out.

Be brave Melissa.

I opened my mouth again, but still no words. I think I was partially intimidated because my father was sitting in the driver's seat, but I had to do it. I opened my mouth again, and out came,
"Mommy, can cousins get married?"

There was an awkward pause; either that or time froze. Either way, I held my breath because I didn't know what the repercussions of that question would be.
My mother just calmly replied,
"No, they cannot."

Conversation Over

Instantly, relief rushed over me. Yes! I didn't have to get married. I didn't envision my 'forever' with him. I could push it out of my mind and try to have the normal life that I craved so badly.

That flashback brought some very troubling questions to mind. As a parent myself, had my child asked me a question like that, after giving the response my mother did, my follow up question would be,

"Why would you ask a question like that?"

Followed by,

"Did something happen?"

Quite frankly, 6-year-olds have pretty vivid imaginations, but that doesn't mean their questions should be taken lightly. I was concerned that my father didn't voice his opinion.

Why didn't he say anything?

Most, if not all fathers, are very protective of their daughters and I believe that question should have sparked a conversation.

Why didn't they see the signs?
Why would a 6-year-old want to marry their cousin?

Their lack of parental concern elevated my parenting skills. Their experience as parents was my instruction to do better. My greatest fear since then has been not being in tune with my son. I understand that as the generations progress, there will always be a thing or two that will fly right over my head, but I cannot afford not to know my child. I don't know if my parents ever spoke to each other about that question, but I indirectly cried for help, and they left me stranded. My parents didn't know that their 6-year-old was molested.

Their lack of parental concern elevated my parenting skills. Their experience as parents was my instruction to do better.

My therapy sessions helped me come to terms with many situations in my life. For a very long time, a statement that my mother made to me when I was 12 left me perplexed. At that age, just like any other pre-teen, I was slowly weaning myself away from my parents, and I was trying my very best to be as independent and resilient as possible. So independent that I thought that I could hide intricate details of my life from them. When I saw my period for the very first time (November 28, 2003), I intended to keep it a secret for as long as I could. I wanted to prove a point – my parents didn't know anything about me.

It was the evening of a friend's birthday party. I was getting ready to jump in the shower and BAM! There she was. I searched through my mother's cabinet to see if I could steal a few of her hygiene products, a little at a time, and create my secret stash. There was nothing! (Probably because she was 8 months pregnant with my sister).

What was I going to do?

The party would be starting soon, and I needed a pad! I didn't have a choice. I had to call and ask her to bring some home. I called her cell. She picked up on the second ring.

"Mommy, I have to tell you something, but don't tell Daddy."

I thought that my situation was too girly to share with my father. I wasn't ready to tell him. She responded,

"What's wrong?"

"My period started. Can you bring home some products for me? You have none here."

I could hear her as she tried to hold the phone away and told my father that they had to stop by the supermarket and why. This reason was why I wanted to keep things like this away from her. She couldn't keep a secret! It was just like back in the first grade when I told her I had a boyfriend, and I overheard her having a full-blown conversation with one of her girlfriends about it. I was furious. I just wanted to have a regular mother and daughter bond, and she kept ruining it.

The cat was already out of the bag; there was nothing that I could do about it. All I cared about now, was getting to this birthday party. When they came home, my mother unpacked the bags of knickknacks she'd picked up from the store. She pulled out a pack of feminine supplies, threw it to me and said – drum roll please—

"Now I'm gonna see if anyone is touching you."

WHAT?!

Where did that come from?
What was that for?
Who says that to their child?
Did my father hear what she just said?

He probably didn't. That has to be the only logical reason for him not responding. It made no sense to me. This life event would have been a teachable moment between my daughter and I, had I been in my mother's shoes. She made me extremely uncomfortable.

My parents couldn't even sit with me to have 'the talk'. They just came home with two books, threw them on my bed and said,

"Here, read this."

My parents were the plug, and I was the socket. We could never function because we could never connect.

They came from a generation where parents and children didn't ever discuss sex or anything sex-related. The thought of having that talk themselves must have been too demanding and educating me through a third party seemed to be the best bet under the circumstances. They were probably scared, but I knew more than they thought. I learned everything about sex – or what I thought sex was – from school.

What was going on in my parent's head?

*Why did they continuously do and say things that
made me look at them differently?
What did I ever do for them to love me like that?*

My parents were the plug, and I was the socket.
We could never function because we could never
connect.

I was depressed about the *As the years*
situation for a while and decided to *passed, I*
stop caring. As the years passed, I kept *kept falling*
falling in and out of love with them. I *in and out*
believed that I didn't know what love
was. I assumed that they didn't know *of love with*
what it was either. I never saw them *them.*
being loving or affectionate towards
each other. The most affection I would
ever see was one parent opening up for an embrace,
and the other pushing him or her away. My brother can
vouch for that! Their disagreements and quarrels were
typical in our house, and the infamous line,

"If I could live my life all over again, I would
never bother with a husband and kids," was often
spewed by my mother. (My brother can attest to that
as well!)

Without my constant effort to maintain my
mental health, I would have probably remained stuck in

confusion. Being able to speak to a professional, about the things that I've endured, provided me with the stability that I needed. Along with my counselor, I had family members who would check in on me from time to time. My father's sister in Jamaica reached out to me a lot after the incident between my father and I. She was genuinely concerned about my well-being. She asked me to tell her what had been happening, and I used the opportunity to vent. I told her everything that was happening at home, both here in the States and in Jamaica, and she was shocked. She asked,

If I could live my life all over again, I would never bother with a husband and kids.

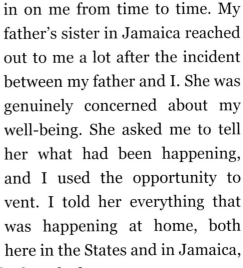

"Melissa if this has been happening all this time, why didn't you say something?"

I couldn't say anything, the treatment I endured from my family was the norm for me. I didn't know that I was being emotionally abused – physically, yes, but emotionally, no. My father's brother had a sit-down with me in 2012 and let me know how much my father loved me, and that he was having a hard time handling me growing up. I couldn't understand how you could love someone and cause them so much pain.

Many other people had their opinions, and only a few were brave enough to have a sit-down with me to figure out what was happening. A family friend, Michelle, privately asked me if my father ever molested me, and at first, I was highly offended.

"He would never!", I screamed in his defense. My father did many things, but molest me, he did not.

Michelle said she only asked because the mannerisms that I displayed were that of a molested individual. I would cringe when she called his name. Any conversation about him would invoke hateful slurs and emotional outbursts. It could be possible that my mannerisms were interpreted that way because I was conditioned to be an abusee.

When I initially decided to go and live with my father, I couldn't go any anywhere without him tagging along. I was once invited to a sleepover, and my father dropped me off and refused to leave. It wasn't so much that he was concerned about my safety because if that were the case, he would have never let me go, to begin with. He was too attached. He treated me like I was his wife.

My mother was no longer putting up with his destructive behavior, so it was my turn to step up to the plate. I was the cook, the cleaner, the laundry person, and the occasional confidante. A few years after I was asked if my father molested me, I nonchalantly told my mother.

"Hey Mommy, someone asked me if Daddy ever molested me. I thought it was absurd!"
Without missing a beat, she asked,
"Well, did he?"
I was shocked. I did not expect that rebuttal from my mother. It made me think deeply.

Why was she so quick to ask that question?
Did she believe that something like that happened between my father and I?
Was this why she was jealous of the relationship I had with my father as a child?

Then it hit me.
She had this thought before.

How could she have an inkling that something like that was possibly happening and not do anything? I was hurt. I was already struggling with emotions of feeling unloved and valueless. Now, I could add a deficiency of protection.

My broken family unit was a big concern for me. I'm the eldest of three who was able to see and understand many things from early on. My brother, and especially my sister, were not privy to many of the things that took place in our home. I used to always worry about my sister's stability.

Unlike my brother and I, she never had the opportunity to understand the dynamic of having her mother and father under the same roof. Another great fear of mine was that she would grow up and attract the same kind of instability that my parents displayed in front of her.

I believe that as the eldest sibling, I have the most significant responsibility to set an excellent example for them. For a while, I felt like I let them down because my life didn't pan out to be the squeaky-clean, Christian-girl, holier-than-thou, cookie cutter life that most people expected from me.

I realized that to be whole, I had to be broken first.

But through my various ups and downs, I realized that to be whole, I had to be broken first, and many of my mistakes proved to be lessons for my siblings.

My inability to make rational decisions stemmed solely from the relationship that I saw between my parents. I struggled for years and rebelled against being just like them. It caused me tremendous suffering because even though I knew they were far from perfect, they wanted me to make God my foundation. They held up their end of the façade by giving me an introduction to God, through church. I was just the wayward sheep that had a problem staying grounded.

CHAPTER 9

Rebellion

I WAS BEYOND lost. Mentally, I was in hell. I was continually going back and forth with my self-worth. I tried to ignore the fact that God was still God and that He would be there every step of the way to protect me, care for me, and love me as no one had ever loved me before.

I was busy focusing on how I could get myself out of the emotional rut I was in. I pushed God to the back burner again and was sort of arrogant with where He stood in my life. I believed that once God calls you, he never deserts you. He's not going to leave you alone until you become obedient to His will for your life. The way I saw it, I would do things my way for as long as I could because God wasn't going to get rid of me until I stopped running and did His will. Ignorantly, I thought I was buying time in my disobedience. However, what I failed to understand was that after a while, God would stop chasing. If I wanted to live like there was no God, He would give me the desires of my heart.

I was His, and He was the only one who ever proudly and consistently claimed me.

As much as I tried to blend in with the world, God had a mark on me - almost like a bright red scarlet letter on my chest. I was His, and He was the only one who ever proudly and consistently claimed me. I realized that, just like Jonah, when God calls you to do something, it doesn't matter how far you run, or how deep you get into things that don't concern you, you can never outrun or hide from God.

I saw the signs, heard His voice, and dismissed almost every person He sent to rescue me. I didn't need Him to save me, as I thought I could sustain myself. Prayers were pointless. I was my own God, and family and friends would never be able to help me the way that I needed.

Deep on the inside, I knew there was a little

light that was very dim, and that light represented the love I had for God. It was smaller than a mustard seed and just needed a little oxygen for that small flame to expand, but I wasn't ready to surrender. I was still too caught up in all the pain and hurt I endured from family, friends, and fellow churchgoers, *I was* and I was not ready to head back to that world. *my*

I believed that if I ever went back to *own* church, I wasn't going back to play around. I *God.* was going to be real with God and allow His grace and love to shine through me. I wanted to be the definition of a testimony. I didn't want to serve God with one foot in the church and one foot in the world. That approach was hypocritical, and I knew that God desired holiness and truth – something I couldn't (or wouldn't) commit to. In the past I was labeled as a radical – I'd do something really well, or really badly. There was no middle ground and serving God would be no different.

I wanted to party, get drunk and high, and try to forget about whatever problems I was having. Me occasionally going to church was to feel some kind of love from God, but as much as I tried, church felt forced and insincere. Church just didn't seem like the place for me to be. There were so many things that pushed me away, like my parents' separation. It infiltrated the sanctuary and was the talk of the town both here in the States, and back home in Jamaica. It also didn't help that my father was known to have a questionable reputation with women in the church. It made me question the type of God I was supposed to

It made me question the type of God I was supposed to be serving and the type of Christian that I had to be.

be serving and the type of Christian that I had to be.

How could I stay in an atmosphere like that?

How could I hold my head up and walk in confidence?

I found myself struggling with living to please people. I would say that my main focus was God and building a relationship with Him, but the truth was that I got caught up in so much church drama that I forgot my soul purpose.

My intent was never to stray too far away. I wanted to be lukewarm – far enough to have my fun, but close enough to jump back in if things got too crazy. I didn't understand how vicious sin could be. It is never as pretty as it appears to be. Sin is like a Tootsie Pop – nice and sweet on the outside, but chewy, sticky, and confusing on the inside.

To convince myself that staying away from

church was right and necessary, I'd use the fact that I didn't have much of a testimony. I'd see church members express some of the hardships they'd been through and how God made a way for them, and all I could say was:

"He woke me up this morning and put me in my right mind. He put food on my table and shoes on my feet".

My testimonies felt dry and weak. They were boring and would be expected from a 6-year-old, but not a 20-year-old. I didn't understand that my testimony, even though it was small, was still significant, because it was confirmation that God was in my corner, protecting me from the wilds of this cynical world. He was my hedge, but I was too stubborn to notice.

My focus was to go out to nightclubs and lounges. I wanted to lose control. I wanted the typical secular, coming-of-age type of lifestyle. I wanted real friends outside of the four church walls. These would be the people, my people, who I could be worldly with, without fear of judgment. I wanted my freedom. I wanted this feeling to last forever - but it didn't.

During my downward spiral, I'd feel a tug at my heart, and I knew it was God. Slowly, the things that

I once found joy in started to become unpleasant to me. No matter how hard I tried to dig my heels deeper into the party life, I could not find any joy or peace. I figured there was nothing else to do but stick to the things I knew. I fought the desire to go back to church for months. During the week, I would get excited about going back, and by Saturday night/Sunday morning, I had found a way out. At first, the excuses were school-related, and I pledged to do things differently once I graduated. When I graduated, I just needed a break from the hustle and bustle of the week; I needed Sunday to be my rest day, and as you'd guess, the excuses kept piling up.

There was one week where I couldn't continue to lie to myself anymore; because that's the only person I was fooling. I got myself together and went to church, and it felt good! But not good enough to hold and convict me the way I'd hoped.

I depended on the pastor's word to convict and paralyze me with the fear of God. This common misconception is what allows many people to walk away and stay away. We sometimes feel that it is the pastor or preacher's responsibility to get us to that place, where we feel so full that nothing else matters beyond God. That's not their responsibility. That's ours! We are responsible for our own salvation, and we are required to figure it out with fear and trembling.

I didn't want to study God's Word for myself. I wanted it handed to me. I was thrust into pure confusion, and the basis of my faith was shaken. I struggled with believing and separating truth from fiction. I even got to the place where I questioned His entire existence.

Was what I was taught for all those years true?
Was this an old fable created by slaves to empower their fellow man through hard times?
Was this a made-up story by white men, to keep minorities oppressed?
Was there really a Heaven and a Hell?
How do we know for sure what happens when we die?

I wanted solid, tangible confirmation that all this was for real. I spent years in school studying finance, and there was always substantial evidence to back up any claim. 2 x 2 = 4. Getting any other answer was impossible.

With God, that unmistakable evidence was not all there. All I had to go by were stories written in a book. I've never seen this man, nor do I know anyone who has. My belief was supposed to be rooted in faith – the substance of things hoped for, the evidence of things that I cannot see. But I couldn't see it, and because I could not see it, I could not understand it. Because I could not understand it, I did my own thing.

I was miserable, and I refused to admit that to myself. I kept pushing against the grain and forcing myself to believe that this was a godless world. I partied harder, I drank more, and I entertained the wrong crowd, more intensely than I ever had before.

My 21st birthday was a milestone that required an ultimate celebration. That is what I told myself after experiencing the disappointments of not celebrating my birthday since the age of 7. I remember sincerely wanting a Sweet 16 and being disappointed when those dreams shattered.

Almost every girl dreams of the day they walk into semi-adulthood. That transition is usually acknowledged with a Sweet 16 soiree. For most, a stunning venue had to be selected, a theme set, guests would be invited, and everything would be topped off with an elegant dress and an astounding entrance, with a handsome young man in tow.

I went as far as making a guest list and creating a theme. I knew that I wanted to wear a black and yellow dress that was cut right above the knees and flared, creating a poof effect. It had laced sleeves that stopped right below the elbows, and the top was laced at the neck with a Cinderella neckline bustier underneath.

The dress would be accompanied by a pair of yellow stilettos and a matching clutch, and as the intro to Stevie Wonder's "Isn't She Lovely" started to serenade the guests, I'd slowly make my entrance escort in tow and wow the crowd.

What was I thinking? Which proud Pentecostal family was going to allow their supposedly saved daughter to wear what I just described and play secular music? Certainly not mine! (Even though my father listened to secular music, I doubt he'd allow it in front of his prominent church friends).

I started making mental notes about my Sweet 16 as early as I could. As the time drew closer and closer, I had to swallow the pain I felt when I realized it was never going to happen. As a means to keep myself from dying on the inside, I shifted my focus to an Elegant 18. It would be more sophisticated – my transition into womanhood. Not much on my list would change, so I'd hold on to that three-ringed binder paper for future reference.

Then my 18th birthday came and went, and there was no party. It was unclear if my parents even tried to put something – anything together for me. I held on to that piece of paper for years hoping that someday someone would surprise me with a special day.

When my 21st birthday rolled around, I wasn't

waiting for my parents to throw me a surprise party. In fact, by the time I was 21, I had no relationship with either parent. I knew that the party that I was dreaming of would have to come from me. So, what did I do for my 21st birthday you ask?

A friend, Chanel, and I threw a house party in Brooklyn. We invited other friends and planned to party until the sun came up, or the cops were called – whichever came first. We played music, that I'm sure upset the neighbors, and danced for hours. For me, the best part was drinking. Thinking back, I may have had a mild drinking problem I've always shown interest in liquor and wine. As a child, the closest I'd been to liquor was the bottle of Alize in my parents' fridge that I stole and replaced with water, hoping they'd never notice.

Dark liquor wasn't one of my favorites. I couldn't get accustomed to the harshness I felt as it went down my throat and burned my stomach. Nobody taught me that drinking on an empty stomach was a no-no. I didn't know that mixing light and dark liquor was a recipe for disaster, but it felt so good every time I did it. That mixture was my drug of choice. I was ready to have a good time and prove to everyone that I was no lightweight and that I couldn't get drunk.

"It's just not in my nature," I'd say.

That night I drank, and drank, and drank some more. And the same friends I boasted to about never being drunk, wanted to test my theory and I took the bait – without pushback. They gave me shot after shot. I downed more than half a bottle of Hennessy and finished a bottle of Cîroc Cotton Candy. I took a couple of shots of Patron and Absolut, then had a beer or two, and sipped from anything else that was behind the bar. All of this in the space of 2 hours. I felt fine – a little tipsy, but fine. I needed to drink more. I took more shots of Cîroc and kept my salt and lime handy.

After a few more rounds, things became hazier than I was accustomed to, but I couldn't tell my friends that I was starting to break. I had to be tough. So, I doctored a small drink and continued partying. One of my coworkers, Mason, showed up to the party, and when he saw me, he asked if I was ok. My response:

"Of course. You know I don't get drunk."

We laughed and chatted for a while, and that's when everything changed.

The room started spinning, I started slurring my words, and my motor skills were shutting down. My hand-eye coordination was poor, and many things appeared to be closer than they really were. I needed to get it together. I sat next to Mason, and once again, he asked,

"Are you ok?"

"Yeah, I'm good. I just need a little break."

"Wait a minute! Are you drunk?"

"Pshhh of course not. I just need some water."

I got the water, drank the entire bottle, and suddenly didn't feel well. I figured because it was late, and I had been up working all day and partying all that night, I should probably take a nap to recuperate. I went to the restroom, relieved myself and went to my friend's bedroom and tried to sleep the liquor off. I tossed and turned for what felt like an eternity. I couldn't understand why I felt the way I did. My heart was racing, and my breathing was staggered. The feeling grew progressively worse.

And then I was out.

I slowly opened my eyes. Rays of sunshine penetrated the curtains. Horns were blowing in the distance and my head felt like it was being pounded. In all my life, I've never felt pain and discomfort the way I did that day. I didn't have enough energy to get myself up out of bed.

Oh my God, am I paralyzed!
Why can't I speak?
Why is my throat so dry?
What happened last night?

But the thing that scared me the most was that I was wearing an entirely different set of clothes than the ones I'd gone to sleep in. I began to worry.

Why were my clothes changed?
Who changed me?
Why is the house so quiet?
Where is everybody?

I mustered up some strength. I had to see what was left of the party. I dragged myself out of bed and made my way to the living room.

EMPTY

Everyone was gone. The house was spotless!

Is this where the party was?

"Hey there, party girl!" my friend said, shouting

from the kitchen.

"How are you feeling?"

"I'm weak and thirsty," I muttered, while rubbing my temple.

"And it looks like you've got a hangover too."

I groaned.

"I thought you said you couldn't get drunk?"

"I can't," I responded defensively.

"Not according to my sheets."

"What?"

I could have died in my mess – literally!

"You blacked out and threw up all over my sheets. I came looking for you and found you swimming in your vomit. If you weren't lying on your stomach, you would have probably drowned in it".

This girl had a good heart because after describing all of the damage I had caused, she still felt the need to take care of me. She changed the sheets, changed my clothes, and made sure I slept comfortably for the rest for the night/day (I still can't remember what day it was). I'm not sure if I'd do that for anyone. I was speechless and embarrassed.

How did I allow myself to stoop this low?

I was fighting to get approval from people, many of whom don't even speak to me anymore. I could have died in my mess – literally! All because I was more focused on fitting into a scene that was not for me.

But the more I pushed myself into that light, the more bound I became.

✥

How much longer was I willing to lie to myself?
How much more of my time was I willing to waste while God patiently waited for me to get my act together?

I was fighting with myself on the inside, and still, there was no break on the outside. I'd convinced myself that this lifestyle was normal, and all my friends did it, so why should I try to be different.

I pushed the quiet little voice inside of me deep into the bottom of my heart. I didn't want to be a boring church girl. I wanted to have fun and be free. But the more I pushed myself into that light, the more bound I became. Even after all that mess, I couldn't and wouldn't change. This is the life had I wanted to live, and I was going to grab it by the shoestrings and keep pushing.

I was still focused on my schooling and wanted to be successful in the banking world. I was confident I could do it all on my own – pass all my classes and get that dream job on Wall Street straight out of college. I was going to make it because deep down, I knew whose I was, but not who I was. And I believed that knowing whose I was would get me through life, almost effortlessly. It was more of a struggle than I was willing to admit. The classes were long and tedious, and every time I thought I was closer to graduation, something changed. I couldn't give up; I had to get my degree. It was expected of me. I had to prove that my whole life wasn't a mess. I depended on that degree to attain my goals, and right when I thought things couldn't get any worse, I found out I was pregnant.

Deep down, I knew whose I was, but not who I was.

CHAPTER 10

Fatal Destination

MY EARLY TWENTIES were rough. I buried myself in parties all while looking for the one. Every snake I'd kiss would turn into a frog and the idea of having a happily ever after seemed out of reach. So, I gave up looking for long term love and started looking for short term lust.

I met a gentleman, Trevor, who frequented my job. He was tall and slender with memorizing eyes. After some time, I realized that the attraction was mutual. He would call my job, ask for me, inquire about a product, stop by to see said product, but spend all his time trying to gain my attention.

All my coworkers noticed and soon, it would become standard for Trevor to stop by my job and take me on short lunch dates. This friendship was slowly starting to blossom into something more, and it started eating away at one person – my boss, Kevin.

Kevin always despised Trevor and consistently made remarks about me finding someone better. Trevor was a gentleman. I couldn't understand why Kevin was so bitter about it.

Over the next few months, things began to get strange. Outside of school, Trevor had a side job as a photographer. Regardless of what he did in life, being a photographer was his passion and would always be a primary source of income. On the surface, that seemed entirely reasonable, but his specialty was female nudity.

I was not pleased with that. There was no way I would seriously consider being in a relationship with someone who wanted to make a career out of being around naked women, and who felt comfortable with women posing in compromising positions to get the perfect shot. I spoke to him about my concerns and was labeled a conservative and that I should understand that nothing has ever or would ever happen. That was not the response I expected, but I felt that he would change over time.

Meanwhile, on the job front, my boss Kevin was

allegedly fired for performance. The team believed his termination was unjust and was based on the color of his skin. He was the last African American manager in the district, and the new Hispanic district manager was getting rid of all the African American managers and replacing them with Hispanic managers.

My coworkers and I didn't know how to handle the change without jeopardizing our jobs. So, they stayed silent.

Kevin reached out to me for help building a court case. Just like the rest of the team, I believed that he was unjustly terminated and decided to put my job on the line to help in any way that I could. I wanted to see him get some justice for the way the company treated him. Almost every day I'd send him new information or call him with news that I had heard.

Me helping Kevin enraged Trevor. He was against me helping my ex-boss. He felt that Kevin liked me and he didn't feel comfortable with us communicating, especially since he was no longer my boss.

I believed Trevor was entirely out of line. I worked with Kevin for a while, and I never once got that vibe. Besides, he was a married man with newborn twins at home. I continued to help Kevin to spite Trevor – just to give him a taste of his own medicine by allowing him to feel the way I felt about him working with naked women.

Kevin and I remained in contact for a while. Eventually, he began confiding in me about things that were happening in his home. He complained about how childish his wife was and how their relationship lacked effective communication. Whenever he'd try to talk to her, she'd throw a fit and start crying.

She'd often leave the responsibilities of the home on him, and after a long day of work, he'd come home to a dirty house, no dinner cooked, and two babies screaming for affection. He felt that he was carrying his marriage by himself and was frustrated. Kevin found himself spending less time at home and more time out with his friends.

Christmas was around the corner, and my coworkers wanted to do something special for our ex-boss. We all put money together, bought him a gift, and invited him to our Christmas party. He was flattered that we thought so highly of him and gladly accepted our invitation.

Fast forward to the night of the Christmas party. I spent the afternoon on a date with Trevor. We went to see a movie, walked around New York City until it was time for me to get to my company's party. He graciously escorted me to the door of my office. Then he saw Kevin, and our evening turned for the worse.

"Why is he here!", he yelled.

"My coworkers invited him", I replied.

"I don't feel comfortable with this. I'm coming to your Christmas party!", he demanded.

"No, you're not!", I screamed at him.

"I don't like the idea of him being at an office party with you. I don't trust him. I know he likes you!"

That was the last straw for me. I had had it with Trevor and his insecurities. I believe that whenever anyone is so insecure, it is because they are guilty of indiscretions themselves.

"I have had it with your jealousy! It is ok for you to be around naked women for a living, but me going to a Christmas party with my ex-boss and coworkers is a bad thing?", I yelled.

"I don't trust him!", he fired back.

"That's fine! You can stay out here and not trust him all by yourself!", I concluded, and with that, I never spoke to Trevor again.

I was so annoyed with all the things Trevor would say about Kevin. The last thing I wanted was a jealous and controlling boyfriend.

I walked into the office with all eyes on me.

"What was that about?", my assistant manager Roger asked.

"Nothing Roger", I replied as I stormed off.

I could hear the whispers and chatter as everyone slowly moved on from the awkward scene I had just presented to them. Roger and Kevin looked at each other with smirks on their faces and mumbled incoherently.

I stayed away from my coworkers until we all decided to go bowling. The bowling alley was not too far from my workplace, so walked and smoked. Marijuana wasn't new to me. It wasn't my go-to drug, but I needed it to get the edge off from this uneventful evening.

"So, what happened with your boyfriend?", Kevin asked as he slowed his stroll to walk with me while passing me the blunt.

"He was not my boyfriend, and I ended that friendship."

"Why?"

"Because he's not what I'm looking for."

"What are you looking for?"

I cautiously looked at him through the side of my eye.

Before I could properly respond, we had arrived at the bowling alley.

We had a blast that night. I had forgotten all about my earlier woes, and I was ready to call it a night. At that time of the night, no one was going home by themselves. We all grouped up based on where we lived and traveled home together. There were only two people who lived close to me; Janet and Kevin. Kevin had driven that day, which meant we'd get home in 45 minutes. It would have taken us 3+ hours to get home on public transportation.

On the drive home, we decided to stop to get some breakfast (it was about 4 a.m.). We went to a local diner where we laughed, talked and reminisced about things that happened at work over the last few months. Janet's attitude started to change.

"Girl, what's wrong?", I asked.

"My boyfriend is flipping out," she responded.

"About what?"

"He wants to make sure that Kevin drops me home before he drops you off."

Confused, I asked her why and she explained.

"My boyfriend doesn't trust Kevin. He feels like

Kevin will try to make a move on me."

Were all these guys just insecure or did they really think that Kevin was that kind of guy? Yes, he was an attractive man, but he was married, with newborn twins at home!

To prevent any issues in her relationship, she requested to be dropped off first. We paid our bills and left. I knew how fragile Janet's relationship was and I prayed that our outing wouldn't make matters worse.

Within 10 minutes of leaving the diner, we were at Janet's apartment. She swiftly said her goodbyes, and then there were 2.

I didn't feel uncomfortable hanging out with Kevin by myself; after all, it wasn't our first time. We'd spend hours at a time talking to each other about life and the troubles we faced. It was safe to call him a friend.

We got to my house, he dropped me off and left. Perfect day, right? Wrong! I left my shoes in his car, and if his wife was anything like he explained, I needed those shoes back - tonight! I frantically rushed through my purse trying to find my phone. He picked up on the second ring.

"Kevin, you have to turn around."

"Why?" he asked.

"I left my shoes in your car, and I don't want any problems."

"Problems with who?"

"Look, just bring my shoes back please."

"I'll only bring your shoes back if you'll give me a kiss."

"A what?"

"A kiss. A kiss for your shoes".

"Just bring my shoes, please. Thanks bye".

Janet's boyfriend and Trevor could see Kevin for who he really was. He was an unfaithful man, who started trouble any opportunity he could. Too bad I wasn't smart enough to realize that I was about to walk into the fire. Bringing those shoes back, or forgetting them in the first place, was one of the biggest mistakes I've ever made in my life.

As a young, naive, immature girl, the fact that an older man was interested in me, stroked my ego. Immediately, whatever morals I had left was tossed through the window.

He got back to my house within 10 minutes, gave me my shoes and requested his kiss. This was the opportunity for me to shut him down and dismiss him, but I didn't. We both went in for the kiss, and my life instantly changed.

⌣

I went back to my house, and I couldn't look myself in the mirror. I knew better.

Why did I fall for this?

Even after all of this, I never cut ties with Kevin. The phone calls and the texts kept coming. Then the gifts and trips started. He was spending more time with me, and less with his family. For 20-year-old me, that attention felt good, but I was selfish and didn't think about the ramifications of my actions.

I didn't make any vows, so it's not my problem.

The longer the conversations and the attention, the deeper I got caught in this web of deceit. I was on a train that was leading straight down a hill, and the thought of pulling the emergency brake was the furthest thing from my mind. For the first time in my life, I felt like this affection and attention was what I was missing.

Kevin is nine years older than I am, and his

presence provided me the security that I was yearning for. I felt safe with him. I felt protected by him. These were feelings that were short lived in my childhood. Today, I'd be labeled a home wrecker, or a girl with Daddy Issues - fighting for the love and protection of an older unavailable male figure to fill an emotional void left by a father who was physically present, but emotionally unavailable.

Transitioning through my teenage years, the only man that God placed in my life didn't make me feel safe or secure. I couldn't depend on him, and I wasn't intelligent enough to understand what was happening to me mentally or how it had impacted me at that point in life.

Here I was, playing wife, to a man who was married – to someone else, and a mother to children, who already had a mother.

Things were getting serious, and I believed that Kevin was falling for me. He physically left his wife, got an apartment and asked me to stay with him. The original arrangement was to spend weekends, but we were so inseparable, that I ended up moving in on the spot.

Here I was, playing wife, to a man who was

married – to someone else, and a mother to children, who already had a mother. I didn't think that walking away from his family, to build a relationship with me, was a big deal. Now as I look back, it is safe to say, I was selfish. Besides, if he could so easily walk away from his family (newborns included), there was no reason why he couldn't and wouldn't do the same to me.

But again, my judgment was clouded by the attention, the gifts and the trips. This is what I wanted my whole life, and I wanted it at any cost. Within the first few months, I started talking to Kevin about marriage. There was a small space inside me that believed that to make our situation right we would have to get married. After all, God honors marriages, right?

Kevin at that time had no interest in getting married, he was still legally married and wasn't making any efforts to get a divorce. As time passed, I started to believe that he was taking advantage of me. I thought that Kevin pursued me and wasn't making an effort to make things right. I pushed past my dislikes and discomfort because I couldn't get over the attention he gave me. I convinced myself that I would have my Happily Ever After with Kevin, soon.

One afternoon, I started feeling strange. It felt like something shifted. Kevin and I were hanging out that night, and I told him that I thought I was pregnant.

To avoid further suspicions, we went to the local drug store and bought a pregnancy test. It was probably the only test I've ever been eager to take. The results came back positive, just as I suspected.

Kevin asked,

"Are you sure you want to do this?"

I looked at him confused.

"You have to remember I just had kids, and this may not be the right time to have another."

"What are you trying to say?", I yelled.

"I'm just saying that now may not be the right time."

The audacity of this guy.
How dare he even utter those words.

He was bold enough to make all these moves but suddenly wanted to back out when things got serious.

"Look, I'm having this baby. I don't care about what you have going on. You should have figured that out first", I responded coldly.

I wanted to have a baby, just not under those circumstances. The thought of an abortion was not an option. It was time for us to figure out how to make all of this work because the baby was coming whether or not we wanted it to.

CHAPTER 11

All Change Isn't Bad...Is It?

B EING 21, PREGNANT, unmarried, and degree-less was not the plan I had for my life. This was the complete opposite of what I'd ever envisioned. I've always fantasized about graduating school, getting a great job that paid well, meeting the man of my dreams, falling in love, getting married, having a troop of children, and living happily ever after, in that order – cliché, I know. My reality was not going to change, and there was nothing much that could be done to improve it even if I tried.

All the things that I went through in my life up until that point, taught me to survive, but in actuality, no one had ever shown me to adapt to my reality. I'd run, hide, and deny my problems because that's what I saw throughout my childhood. My family was broken, and issues were never fixed, only rarely addressed. I knew from a young age that that wasn't the life I wanted for myself and that I'd have to push to find "the one" for a few reasons:

1.	To get as far away from the dysfunction as possible.

2.	To build an unbreakable partnership with my spouse as early as possible.

3.	To establish a strong bond with my children.

As if being pregnant, unmarried, and degreeless wasn't enough, I had to brace myself for the worst when it was time to tell my parents. I had just made it through my first trimester, and my doctor informed me that it was safe to let my friends and family know about my good news. I knew that my parents would be unhappy, but there was nothing that could be done in this situation. It was time, and I had to let them know.

I sat my mother down and told her that I had some news to share. She looked at me a little confused, wondering what little secret I had up my sleeve.

"Mommy, you're going to be a grandmother."

"What?"

"I'm pregnant."

"How far along are you?"

"Just a little over three months."

"When did you find out?"

"Just over two months ago."

"Honestly, I thought you were going to tell me you were graduating early."

I could hear the disappointment in her voice.

"I know, Mommy."

"Well, what's done is done. Did you tell your father?"

"No. I'm going to tell him now."

"So, who is the gentleman? Do I know him?"

"No, Mommy."

"Well, you need to bring him by so I can meet him."

"Okay, Mommy."

We chatted for a few minutes more, and for the first time ever, we had a mother and daughter conversation, one that I'd longed for all my life. It was refreshing. I felt love.

Next was my father. I knew that this was going to be a little tricky. I never expected there to be any congratulations from him. I decided to tell him, not because I needed to, but because there was still some shred of decency still left in me and I didn't want him to hear from someone else. I dialed his number. The phone rang three times.

"Hello?"

"Hi Daddy."

"Hey, what's going on?"

"I have some news to share with you."

"What's that?"

"You're going to be a grandfather."

"What do you mean?"

"I am pregnant."

"What do you mean you're pregnant?!"

Silence. I didn't know how else to spell it out.

"If you knew you were going to be engaging in that type of behavior, why didn't you use protection?

"What?" was all I could say.

The same man who couldn't sit down to discuss puberty with me suddenly wanted to discuss safe sex.

"Do you know how much of an embarrassment you're going to cause me?"

Did he just say what I thought he said?

"I can't believe this! How am I going to explain this to people?", he continued.

"It's not for you or anyone else to explain. I am

the one that will be walking around with a baby in my stomach."

I wasn't concerned about what people would think. The way I saw it, the only person I needed to explain myself to was God. My father and I talked for a little while longer, mostly about how my pregnancy was going to affect him. He went into great detail about the apartment he wanted my son's father to provide for me. He wanted to know when the gentleman and I were going to get married. He even went as far as asking if the gentleman had any college degrees. If everything would go according to my father's plan, his reputation would be saved.

I didn't think any of that mattered at the moment. All that mattered was me having a healthy and safe delivery. I made it very clear to my family, my father especially, that if they weren't there to support me through the pregnancy, they should not show up when my child was born. My father thought I was joking. I didn't speak to him again for a while.

I remember going through my pregnancy quietly because I wanted to enjoy every moment. Whether I was married or not didn't change the fact that there was a beautiful life developing inside me.

Then came the delivery. I woke up around 5 a.m. on Saturday, October 26, 2013, with contractions. The contractions didn't last very long but they felt extremely uncomfortable, and I knew that my baby was coming sooner than later. At this point, I was exactly one week shy of my due date, so I knew that anything was possible. Kevin was well aware of what was happening but insisted that he had to go to work. No begging and pleading would help my case.

Off to work he went, leaving me alone with contractions, the fate of our unborn child, and his one-year-old twin boys. I knew that I was going to give birth that day, and with the contractions lasting longer and coming quicker, I could not take care of his children. I needed help. I was in too much discomfort to think about the children.

By 2 pm that afternoon, the contractions were 5 minutes apart, lasting for about 45 – 60 seconds. In other words, I was getting ready to push. I called my mother and brother who came to assist me. I called Kevin at work, and let him know that under no circumstances, was I planning to have the baby at home (I wanted the epidural) and if he wasn't home soon, I'd call the ambulance.

About 15 minutes later, Kevin got to the house. There was no time to exchange pleasantries. We gathered my things and headed to the elevators. I felt strong enough to walk and did pretty well, but that wait for the elevator felt like an eternity had passed. As soon as the elevator got to our floor, I fell to my knees in the most agonizing and excruciating contraction of the entire pregnancy. Kevin was more concerned with getting on the elevator and began pulling my arm to get me to move. I screamed at him telling him to stop, while my mother explained that he had to wait for the contraction to pass.

After about 50 seconds, I was back on my feet, wobbling towards the car. I grew impatient as I sat in the front seat of his 2013 Honda Accord, waiting for him to load the kids in the back of the car. Seeing all of what was happening, my brother decided to come to the hospital with us, but my mother decided to go to work. I tried hard not to think about it, but on the drive to the hospital, I was horrified. I didn't know what to expect next. Deep inside, I wanted my mother to be there to hold my hand and encourage me. This was my first child, her first grandchild, and I didn't think I needed to ask her to come. That resentment quickly disappeared when the next round of contractions hit.

By the time I was admitted to the labor and delivery ward, I was dilated enough to start pushing. After three pushes, my little prince came into this world, quietly. No crying, no screaming, no sound. The doctors prepared me for that possibility, so I was not stunned. They took him, cleaned him up, gave him a shot, and for the first time, I heard my son's voice; I wept uncontrollably.

I cried because I'd made the transition into motherhood and I was happy, yet utterly clueless about what was to happen next. I realized that my parents were not going to be there the way that I wanted them to be, and this fueled the postpartum depression that I was unaware that I had. I was alone on my journey with only the support of Kevin.

It was hard in the beginning, but as time went on, I learned how to grasp the basics of parenting and decided then and there that I had to do things differently from my parents. I had to be there for my son and develop a bond with him; unlike the one, I had with my parents. It was a fight from the very beginning to end the dysfunction that I was so used to living in. But this fight would prove hard to accomplish.

Dysfunction was typical; it was second nature back home in Jamaica. I watched how my parents treated each other, and I was determined at a very young age that I was not going to have the type of relationship that they did.

Based on their dysfunction, I began my quest for love as a teenager. I started looking for love. In my head, I believed it wouldn't be difficult at all. I'd just meet someone who had the same intentions I did, and the rest would be history. I didn't understand why grownups had difficult relationships if they indeed married their soulmates. So, the quest began. I really thought I could do it.

But what I didn't know was that I couldn't do anything, especially on my own. Without God in the center of everything I set out to do, nothing would flourish. Anxiety consumed every aspect of me because my only plan was failing. All I wanted to do was to build a better life than the one I had.

All I wanted to do was to build a better life than the one I had.

At the age of 14, I submerged myself in what I thought was a serious relationship with a young man, Mike, who was two years my senior. He was the man whom I believed would become my husband. However, there was a tiny problem.

In the beginning, I felt like Mike wasn't as transparent as I'd hoped he'd be. This was a serious matter for me, and I paid close attention to all the signs that would appear.

After dating for almost two years, I found out that when Mike was still with his ex-girlfriend when he started dating me. I couldn't ignore this. I was always the best two years of my life! (Yes, I spoke like I was a grown woman with an extensive list of life experiences). I confronted him about it and with one of the most defeated looks on his face, he explained,

"Yes, it's true, but..."

"But what!?"

There was nothing in the world that he could say or do to get out of this debacle. His excuse was that he liked me a lot and he didn't want me to lose interest in him because he was with someone else.

WHAT?
Should I be angry about this?
Should I just accept it?

This relationship was the only one that I knew, and I had to preserve it. This was the first dysfunctional relationship, outside of my parents, that I was involved with. We were young, but I submitted myself to the confusion because the last thing I wanted was to date a long list of church guys before I could find Mr. Right. This was supposed to be a fairytale. We were supposed to fall in love and live happily ever after.

If I knew what Kevin did from the beginning, I would never have dated him. His actions made me feel stupid – like I was being used. It made everything clear to me though. I used to see his ex-girlfriend all the time around our church, and she would always have the meanest look on her face when she saw me; I could never understand why. I figured she was just upset because Mike moved on with me. She would get over it, eventually. I wasn't going to allow her feelings to dictate how my life with him was going to turn out. I was grown, and this young man was going to be my high school sweetheart. I had a bright future planned out for us.

This relationship was a little frustrating, but I figured these were the hard times that grown-ups often referenced. I felt that I needed to trust Mike and accept his forced honesty as a form of transparency. This little bump in the road will bring us closer together.

If I didn't want my relationship to be like my parents', it was off to a very rocky start. I didn't realize that it takes a lot to have a healthy relationship.

About a year later, I went to Mike's school barbecue to hang out with him and our mutual friends. After being there for only a few hours, he mysteriously disappeared. I called, no answer. I texted him, and he said he would meet up with me in a few minutes. A few minutes turned into an hour. An hour turned into 2. It was a red flag, but I had no way of proving my suspicions. I tried to stay positive and occupy myself with my friends.

Then my phone rang. It was a good friend of mine, Charlie, who attended the same school that Mike did. He knew Mike and I were dating, so it was no surprise for him to see Mike there. Charlie said,

"Melissa, I was trying to get your attention. You and Mike just ran past me."

That was strange because, at that time, I wasn't with Mike. I was with my friends.

"Are you sure it was me?", I asked.

"Yes, you're wearing a red dress..."

Everything Charlie said after that was a blur. I wasn't wearing red; I was wearing green. This was getting out of hand. I needed to track Mike down. I walked around that venue, between partygoers, up to the stage where all the artists performed, only to run into his ex - in the red dress. I shook my head in disbelief and headed for the exit. It all started making sense now. I had all the answers I needed. That was the beginning of the end.

How could someone whom I cared for so much do something so horrifying to me? I needed to change my dependency. I depended on him not to hurt me. I depended on him to stick to my plan. I depended on him to want a forever with me. That hurt stemmed from my need to be in control, which in turn originated from what I thought relationships were supposed to be. I didn't realize that, at 14 years old, it was nearly impossible to have it all figured out. I was extremely hard on myself, and it took me a while to let that stress go.

Although he and I didn't officially call it quits until quite sometime after that, I had already moved on in my mind and my heart. I realize now, that the pain that was inflicted on me by Mike, I later transferred to Kevin's wife.

DISCLAIMER: Mike and I have grown a lot since then. Today, we are still friends who look at the past and chuckle at the decisions we made as children. We have nothing but mutual love and respect for each other.

Throughout my years, I've encountered many friendships and relationships and was dissatisfied with how many of them left me dry or were pointless. I was able to pen my feelings and thoughts and came up with this:

I Want More

I've always given myself wholeheartedly to love.
But always felt like something was missing in return.
I get it; there are no two people who are alike
So, I'm not expecting perfection.
What I want is to be stimulated mentally.

It's like I'm not being challenged enough.
Going through the role is not enough for me.
I want you to get me!
I need you to be intrigued by my complexities.

I want to sit up till the wee hours of the morning debating a TED Talk,
With nothing but pure intellect and mutual respect.

I don't want to be alone with my thoughts anymore.
I want to share them with someone who can understand what drives me.

Looking good isn't enough anymore,
If all that's inside is shallow or void.
I want to be able to use the word perfidiousness,
Without you thinking that I'm talking about your

style.

I can't wait to meet the one that gets me!
Not the cliché type that wants to finish my sentences
and agree with everything I say.
But the one that can truly explain what the purpose of
an electoral college is
Without saying, "It's all set up to fail."
Or the one that can discuss the reality of "soulmates"
When we know "soul-ties" exist.

Most of all, I can't wait to meet someone who can
challenge me with the Word of God.
Let's spend hours using scripture to decipher our true
purpose.
Let's talk about why it's so easy to turn around and
sin again,
After just begging God for forgiveness.
Let's try to figure out why Moses was the only one
who could touch the Ark of the Covenant and survive.
Let's understand what constitutes as a destitute and
reprobate mind.
Explain to me the concept of salvation after reading 1
Corinthians 5:5.

As of now, I will make it my duty to be Intellectually

Stimulated. The days of being mentally alone will all be left in the past.

Yeah, I guess it's ok to talk about what happened on last week's episode of whatever,
But aren't you tired of having meaningless conversations that lead nowhere, with people who don't necessarily care about your well-being?

I say all of this to say; I was hell-bent on making something, that was not meant to be, work. I was resilient in my efforts with Mike, but I had to accept that what God had in store for me would be just right for me. There is nothing that I can do or say about a situation to make it right if it's not mine. I have to be open to change because more often than not, my plans fail, and I have to adjust to what life throws my way.

I had to accept that what God had in store for me would be just right for me.

It dawned on me as an adult that this dysfunction may be a generational curse. I watched my parents damage each other emotionally, and it felt like I was being dealt the same hand.

All these years later, and the dysfunction seemed to follow me. I was angry at everyone; my parents, my friends, the church, God. I felt that they all had let me down, even though most of them played no direct role in my shortcomings.

I had an excellent excuse for why I didn't complete my degree on time. I felt that I endured traumatic emotional abuse from my father, and it caused me to become depressed – and it did.

My excuse for separating myself from friends was simple. I felt that they weren't all genuine – which they some weren't.

I totally gave up on church because I believed that it was filled with people who pretended to be something they weren't - people who weren't real about their life journey (both good and bad). I felt like church was a scam; a tool designed to keep me in a box. It felt cult-like.

I gave up on God because I assumed that He would give me a good life; bless me with the kind of family that I'd envy from friends

Life came with twists, turns, and derailments, all of which I was susceptible to.

151

and neighbors, bless me with the beauty that I saw in other girls, bless me with friends that weren't seasonal, bless me with the opportunities of a lifetime. Basically, I thought He'd make me and my situation perfect.

I didn't understand that feelings were fickle and changed just as often as the weather did.

I failed to realize that life wasn't supposed to be perfect. I didn't understand other people's journey. It was wrong for me to judge their lives, instead of working to fix mine. Life came with twists, turns, and derailments, all of which I was susceptible to. I was not above the problems that life brought. I didn't finish my degree on time because I allowed the influences around me to stop me. My friends weren't genuine to me because I wasn't genuine to them. I walked around with a chip on my shoulder, that same entitlement bug that my father had, thinking and feeling that the world owed me something — not understanding that you reap what you sow; good or bad.

Me giving up on church had a tug on my life for a while. At first, I allowed my feelings to control me. I didn't understand that feelings were fickle and changed just as often as the weather did. If we were all reliant on said feelings, we would all make decisions that would lead to rash consequences. Whenever I didn't feel like going to church, I'd just not show up. Every week was accompanied by excuses that lead nowhere. Eventually, I sunk to the depths of unbelief and stayed there for a long time. I wasn't sure if what I'd been taught all those years was just a figment of my imagination, passed down from one generation to the next.

I wanted a shortcut to God.

I didn't believe anymore because I wanted to see proof. I wanted a shortcut to God. I didn't want to put in the work and see Him manifest. I wanted Him to show and prove Himself to me first. I'd never seen Him, nor did I have a close enough relationship to feel Him the way I heard others did. There were points in my early relationship with Him where I thought I felt Him, but after a while, it felt like the relationship became one-sided, with me making all the effort to make things work. After not seeing the results that everyone else professed, I threw in the towel.

I allowed myself to be influenced by outside factors, like celebrity figures who once walked my walk and believed that something wasn't right, and friends who deciphered things that seemed to make more sense to me. I stopped studying the Word of God for myself. I was lazy with my belief. I wanted to be taught wisdom and knowledge - I didn't want to do the research and the studying necessary to learn.

So here I was, 21, a new mother, unmarried, degreeless, looking for love and somewhat God-less. Talk about a mess! My life was built on confusion, and I didn't know who or what I could believe in. I knew that a change needed to happen for things to turn around. I just didn't know how to change my situation. I was too proud to ask for help, and I didn't necessarily believe that prayer was the answer. I felt like maybe if I had to go with the flow and hopefully things would change. After all, if I did good things, I'd receive good things in return, right?

I wanted Him to show and prove Himself to me first.

My first step was transitioning into motherhood. It was one of the hardest things I'd ever done. For over a year, the reality that I was a mother never hit me. I felt like a stranger taking care of someone else's child. Of course, I loved my son, but it just didn't feel like the love a mother would have for a child. He didn't feel like mine. These were all side effects of postpartum depression that I was unaware of. In return, I left the brunt of parental responsibility on Kevin. I just didn't know how to be a mom. I was too busy trying to finish school and get ahead in Corporate America. I didn't have time to figure that part out. I just assumed that if it were meant to be, the nurturing part of me would come about - eventually.

If struggling to be a mother was difficult then, it became even more difficult when we found out I was pregnant again. At this point, our son was a year old, and the tension between Kevin and I was beginning to rise. I knew the moment I became pregnant. I could feel it. I told Kevin right away, and we agreed on taking a home test to confirm my belief. It was positive. I was happy, but I was depressed. I had just gone back to school, and I wanted to complete my degree badly. At that time, the only person I felt I could talk to was Kevin, but he was not very receptive of my thoughts or feelings. Kevin put his foot down. He did not want to have another, not now at least. He made it very clear when he reminded me that he didn't want to have the first, much less a second, and piggybacked of my zeal to finish school, as an excuse not to have another.

In an attempt to make him happy, and to try to keep things going good at home (after all, I wanted that engagement ring), I followed along, and at 9 weeks, on July 3, 2014, I regrettably had an abortion and found myself in a deeper and darker depression than I ever had in my life. There is no worse feeling than looking at the tiny corpse whose life was snuffed out because of my foolishness and selfishness. I stared at the baby that I should have protected. I called out to Kevin to show him what should have been our child. He came, saw the baby, apologized and walked away.

There was no comforting.

There was no regret.

He did not care.

I had to pull myself together. If Kevin wasn't going to comfort me, I knew that no one else would. I didn't have to listen to Kevin, but I felt I was already deep in this mess of a relationship and I had to make it work, by any means necessary.

This deep secret ate at me for years. I knew of family members and friends, who struggled to have babies, and here I was throwing mine away like a used Kleenex tissue. I hid that pain and cried myself to sleep many nights. Every year since then, around the 4th of July, while everyone else is thinking about food and fireworks, I think about the child whose life I stole and how much I'd give to reverse the hands of time.

My relationship with Kevin did not get better; in fact, it grew worse. I was struggling with the depression of not feeling attached to my child, the deep regret of losing another, and the depression of having to help raise two that weren't mine. I didn't want to feel those feelings anymore, so I distracted myself by getting into grad school and started my master's program the same month I received my bachelor's degree. Kevin was forced to bathe the kids, feed them, and play with them. I hardly did any of it.

I was struggling with the depression of not feeling attached to my child, the deep regret of losing another, and the depression of having to help raise two that weren't mine.

My physical appearance began changing drastically. My usual weight of about 125 pounds dropped to a solid 95 pounds. Whenever I looked at myself in the mirror, I was horrified. I could see my bones poking through my skin. My relationship was weighing on me, and after I graduated in 2016, there was nothing else to distract me from everything at home.

One night, I called my good friend, Cheyanne and vented to her about the situation I was dealing with. I bravely came clean about my situation and about how rocky things were at home. I expounded on my fear of being alone, especially with my son. He still didn't feel like mine. I didn't know how

I was going to get through it on my own. I was going through a lot, and most of my family didn't know the full extent of my situation. So they couldn't provide the support that I needed. Whenever my mother's sister would call to check up on me, I'd feel the need to break down and tell her everything, but I couldn't. I was too afraid.

Cheyanne empathized with me and started sharing some of her experiences. She explained that sometimes it's ok to speak to God, the same way I would have conversations with my friends. She showed me that God understood my heart and that sometimes all I needed to do was open my mouth and tell Him what was wrong. She told me about how she would speak to God aloud in her car while she drove to work and suggested that I give it a try. I was skeptical at first, but with everything around me failing, and my peace of mind diminishing, I figured I had nothing to lose, and it would come in handy on a rainy day.

That day came sooner than I thought. A few mornings after that call, something started brewing inside me. This thing was eating at me for years. It took my joy, and my livelihood and peace were nowhere in sight. I couldn't take it anymore and, while in my car on my way to work, I just exploded, bawling at the top of my lungs. I used that morning to be real with God, and

I poured out my soul in prayer, fully re-surrendering myself to Him.

I told God everything that I did from that night Kevin and I kissed, until that very moment. I told Him how I was feeling. I told Him how much I hated what I was going through now, and how I needed change. I told Him that I saw the error of my ways. And that I no longer wanted to live in my mess, but I wanted to see the blessings He had in store for me. I begged for His forgiveness. It was one of the sincerest prayers I've ever prayed. I took my prayer very lightly. I didn't feel a burden lift off of me after I prayed, until the night when things finally exploded for good.

I was going through a divorce, even though I was never married. Forever turned into never ever, and then there was peace.

A few days after that prayer, Kevin came home, knocked on my room door, and asked to come in. (By this time we no longer shared a bed). He sat at the edge of my bed and with his head in his hands, he explained that he couldn't be in a relationship with me anymore and that he was working on his relationship with his now ex-wife. It was a bittersweet feeling. A part of me wanted our relationship to work. I wanted to have all my children with this man, not because I loved him, but because I wanted all my children to have the same father (something that bothered me for a long time).

He will always do His best to make sure we get the lesson, while He removes our mess to make way for our blessing.

Another part of me took note of how quickly God answered my prayer. I sat there quietly and listened to him justify his decision. I wasn't mad, and I didn't attack him, which surprised us both. Instead, I calmly started making suggestions about next steps. I began taking my name off bank accounts, closing accounts, spitting up assets – I was going through a divorce, even though I was never married. Forever turned into never ever, and then there was peace. It was over, and it was time for me to pick up the pieces. It was time for me to be independent and more than anything, it was time to be there for my son. In the midst of my pain, I became happy. It was an uncomfortable end, but after all, it was what I prayed for.

God doesn't always answer prayers the way we expect Him to, but He will always do His best to make sure we get the lesson, while He removes our mess to make way for our blessing. So be mindful when you pray, because you may receive what you ask for. I believe that God is faithful to those who are faithful to Him and because I opened up my heart to Him, He took care of me.

This was what I needed to get me back on track. It took me some time to realize how bad my relationship was with God, and this was the only way I knew to describe it:

A Love Lost

His mystery was what captivated me.
His love was limitless.
His passion was more than words could describe.
But He just wasn't enough.

Every time I fought to get away,
He'd pull me back in.
And the more He embraced me,
The more I strayed.

With all said and done,
I was trying to close a void,
That only He could fill.

I still felt all alone.
I still felt worthless.
I still wanted more.

I searched high and low,
When all I ever needed
Was right in front of me.

Like the dog with the bone,
Who saw his reflection in the river,
I dived in after what appeared to be greater.
I ran away from the love of my life,
And destroyed the plan He had for me.

Only He would wipe my tears,
When things went south.
Only He would comfort my soul.
Only He would make me whole.

But I realized too late.
He couldn't stick around anymore.
I took Him for granted,
And He left me all alone.

No begging or pleading would change anything.
He was GONE!

Now He's just a distant memory.
A figment of my past.
A love lost.

───※───

As the reality of everything ending began to really sink in, Kevin and I couldn't see eye to eye with many things. For example, he wanted to be with his ex but still live in the home we shared. I wasn't having it. I threw his belongs down the stairs – X-Box included. He wasn't going to have his cake and eat it too - not again.

Today Kevin and I aren't best friends, but we can fully identify that our happiness and our sanity was more important than staying in an unhappy relationship simply because we had a child. Becoming toxic around our son was not an option, so we learned to let go and began new chapters in our lives.

THE LIGHT

CHAPTER 12

Destined to Be Different

WITH ALL THE sudden changes in my life, it was time to walk differently, talk differently, and think differently, but how? I knew there was more to my life than what I was going through. There had to be some form of positivity that I could pull from all this. In the past, I said that I would use my parents' mistakes as learning lessons, but it was easier said than done.

Deep on the inside, something was brewing. I couldn't understand it. It felt like true spiritual, physical, emotional, and financial freedom. I just didn't know how to tap into it. My talents weren't like others; they weren't as visible as those of my classmates and friends from church. Some were born singers and others were great sportsmen. Some were gifted artists while others were dynamic mathematicians. It was clear that many were en route to becoming great doctors and lawyers, and others were bound to be socialites with their effervescent personalities.

I wasn't the greatest student, but I needed to make it. I needed to prove to my parents that I could and would live up to the high expectations they had for me.

I borrowed thousands of dollars in student loans, to complete my education and the reward in the end felt great. I was the only person in my family to complete a master's degree, but on the other hand, I felt incomplete. I was unfulfilled. I wasn't happy.

My passion was my purpose.

Jobs only appeased my need to utilize my degrees for a few months at a time. I needed to find my niche. I needed to find what made me happy, but I didn't know where to look or how to figure it out.

I always felt a calling with reading and writing. As basic as it may seem, it has brought and still brings me happiness. My family never had to pressure me to read a book as a child. Whenever I was too quiet and would seem to be up to no good, I'd be caught in my room engrossed in a good book.

From my elementary school days, my teachers would speak about how beautifully I wrote and how eloquently I spoke. I never thought much of it because I didn't think I could make a career out of writing.

Who would want to read my work?

I didn't believe that my work was unique, but after publishing pieces of my work on a blog I'd created, I began receiving feedback about my writing, and that's when I realized that my passion was my purpose.

Let me pause here to say everyone is born with a gift. It may take a little while before you tap into your true purpose, but you are designed to be the best at whatever you do, and when things don't work out the way you intend, you have to remember that every setback is a setup that God intended for your step up.

Every setback is a setup that God intended for your step up.

So, I decided that I would try my hand at writing and see if there was a future there for me. It also made me think about other aspects of my life. A long period of introspection proved that there were things that I had to work on. The reality is that there will always be things about us that can be improved.

I started controlling my thoughts and the things I would say. I cut all ties with people who were pessimists and respected people for their differences. Things began to change for the better. I applied all my positivity to relationships. I am a firm believer that if you live by the 3 T's—Truth, Trust, and Transparency—your life, and the relationships you'll build, will be seen for what they're worth (I will elaborate on the 3T's in a little while). You will be able to see who's here to stay and who'll be around for a season.

I was able to let go of the need to control situations. Control drained me mentally, physically, and even spiritually. I wanted God to do things on my time. I wanted Him to bless me with a husband at 25 and kids at 26, and everything else in-between. When I was 25 and even 26, I noticed that all the things I wanted didn't come to fruition. It stressed me out and sent my anxiety into overdrive. I wondered if God was even considering blessing me because He did not answer my prayers the way I wanted Him to.

I also stopped worrying about my future. I became content with life as is. I never believed, until that moment, that a life of singleness would bring such joy and peace. Worrying about things I had no control over granted stress a one-way ticket out of my life. Worrying birthed negative energy. It forced me to think about the pros and cons of my situation, and the cons always seemed to outweigh the pros. I now live by the mantra that what God has for me is for me. I believe Him when he says that He'll give me the desires of my heart if I seek Him and His righteousness first.

One of the greatest things that positivity brought to my life was the ability to let go of resentment. All the resentment I held against my parents for years disappeared almost instantaneously, and with it, 150 pounds of stress. I decided I couldn't blame my parents for the way my life turned out. Of course, I wish many things were different, but the reality is that I wouldn't have become half the woman and mother I am today if I didn't have my experiences.

You may be struggling with resentment right now. Resentment is the feeling of being hurt or mistreated. No matter how you try to get rid of that feeling, it always rears its ugly head and builds anger within. Whether it is against family or friends, the damage that comes with resentment will destroy you. Truth is, the past is the past. That was a hard pill for me to swallow. I could not let the past go. It determined how my future played out, I thought, and whenever I felt I got over the resentment, one bad memory would trigger me back into my dark place.

Here's a perfect example: Mike, the gentleman I was dating when I was 14, visited his mom in the States almost every summer. The year I started college, 2009, he came to visit. By then, we weren't together anymore. We still liked each other, but it was clear that a long-distance relationship was not going to work.

Nevertheless, he was here, and I had to see him. Another friend of ours, Paul, was also visiting from Jamaica and was staying at my house with my father, brother and I. Paul's parents had been friends with my parents since my father was in his youth. It was only natural that Paul and I would be friends as well. We all went to the same church and would often spend time with each other. Paul, Mike and I went to Youth Services and Summer Camps and watched each other evolve into young adults.

I told Paul that Mike was in the States and I wanted to see him, but I didn't want to go by myself. Doing that would be a big mistake, especially since we were still attracted to each other. Paul understood and agreed to come with me. We began our 2-hour train and bus commute from Queens, NY to Mt. Vernon, NY, and it was worth it. We reminisced about old times, ate, watched TV, and left.

Fast forward a few days later. It was time for

me to move on campus and start my life as a college student. I was sitting in the kitchen, doing some last-minute packing, when my father stormed in.

"What were you doing in Mt. Vernon?"

"What?", I asked, totally forgetting about the trip.

"You went up there and had sex in Mike's mother's house!"

"What?", This time, it was a question out of confusion.

"That boy will never marry you. No man will ever want to marry you. You went and gave yourself away. You're slack, nasty and loose. I can't even look at you. You're a disgrace and an embarrassment."

I sat there in disbelief.
He didn't ask me anything.
He just attacked.
He didn't give me an opportunity to say anything.
He didn't know if it was true or not; he was just spewing his ugly hate.

He continued,
"I had to call Mike's mother, and she didn't even know you were in her house. You were out there sneaking around doing all sorts of nastiness with this boy. No

one will ever take you seriously. No one will ever want you. You're useless. You make me sick".

Then he walked away.

I sat in the kitchen at a loss for words.

How did he know I went to Mt. Vernon?
Why did he think I had sex?

Then it all started coming to me. The only person who knew that I was going there was Paul. No one else knew. I never mentioned it to anyone, and it never slipped. It wasn't a secret, but I didn't think it was such a big deal that I needed to tell the world.

My confusion slowly turned into anger and hate. Paul was going through his own little dilemma and was trying to get the attention off himself. He was in the States because he had a problem with taking things that didn't belong to him. He was caught stealing money and possessions from many people in our church back home in Jamaica. That news quickly spread to our church in New York, when Paul was accused of stealing a cell phone from a church member. I believed that he probably told my father that lie to avoid being reprimanded for the things he had done.

That whole evening destroyed me. I was doing well at that point in life. I was accepted to an excellent University and was about to start a new chapter, but all my excitement was gone. I sat in the kitchen for about an hour - legs shaking and blood boiling. My father thought less of me because of a lie, and I hated him more every time I thought about how he dealt with me. He never once asked if it was true. He never asked for an explanation. He just looked at me like trash in the street. I reached out to Paul and, to this day, he denies that he ever said anything of the sort to my father. But I knew better. He even went as far as telling his now wife and family that he had sexual relations with me. Clearly, he had a track record that spoke for itself. I realized he was not a true friend, and when that conversation ended, so did our friendship.

A few years after the lie about Mark and I, my brother found himself in a similar situation, and I was waiting to see him get reprimanded. I was sure that my father would have some choice words for him, but instead of being scolded, my brother was praised! He was honored for something that was deemed so wrong, and I was dealt with like a worthless girl with no standards. This anger transformed into bitterness and unforgiveness, and I held on to the hurt for years. Whenever my father's name came up, or whenever someone asked me about him, a fire was rekindled in me and, as time went on, this hurt turned into hate. It drained me. It made me different. It took me years, but in the end, I was forced to realize that resentment causes more hurt to you than the person who hurt you; however, forgiveness is for you and not the person who hurt you. Let it go!

Resentment causes more hurt to you than the person who hurt you; however, forgiveness is for you and not the person who hurt you.

Forgiveness, as I've recently learned, is not easy. Forgiveness isn't about just saying "I forgive you" and moving on with your life. Those words have to match your heart. I was once told that true forgiveness comes when you can speak about the wrongs that happened to you and not become emotional, but I digress. I believe that forgiveness is a process, and even after the process is over, there will be some things that will still hurt. The phrase, "I forgive you, but I won't forget", rings strong. I was forced to believe that all the pain would go away once I said those three words. So, for years, I said those words but didn't mean it.

One instance when I experienced true forgiveness

was when I had a heart-to-heart with my mother about the things that I felt and experienced with her back home in Jamaica. She expressed her sincere apologies because she didn't realize how she affected me. True peace fell over me.

One of the greatest feelings in the world is to have someone understand you and your perspective. I never tried to prove my point to my mother; instead, she was able to see the error of her ways and apologize.

Parents, it may seem hard, or maybe a bit backward, but nothing is wrong with apologizing to your children.

Parents, it may seem hard, or maybe a bit backward, but nothing is wrong with apologizing to your children. We understand that you're in control and you call the shots, but we also know that you're human and you're bound to make mistakes.

The bitterness I had from my parents taught me a precious lesson that I've implemented in the life of my child. If my son feels as though I did him wrong, he can come and express his feelings to me, respectfully. If what he's saying is true, it takes nothing for me to turn to him and say, "You know what? You're right. I could have dealt with the situation this way instead. I'm sorry." Parents, I'm sure you were there once, but let me make it clear. It hurts your children when their feelings and opinions are deemed irrelevant. They have feelings, just like we do.

I didn't believe that my relationship with my mother could heal. After all those years, I didn't realize that all those things still affected me. Deep in my heart, I was holding on to grudges from my childhood.

All those games and events of mine that she missed. All those times when she supported my brother and not me. All the times when she told me I was jealous of all the attention my brother received. It all ate at me, and pushing it out of my head didn't mean that it wasn't in my heart. I had to be honest with myself, and with the person who hurt me, to achieve true forgiveness.

I was once told that the person who angers you, controls you. Can you imagine being mad at 20 people? Those 20 people would have control over you. Think about it—every time you think about those people, see them, hear somebody talking about them, or see their name somewhere, you are giving these people the authority to control you.

They determine whether or not you stay happy or sad. Nothing is wrong with disliking someone because of their character, but you can't hold a grudge against that person for being the way they are. You have to let it go. Your bitterness doesn't affect them - it affects you. You have to be truthful, trusting, and transparent enough with yourself and with others to make it through life.

CHAPTER 13

Truth, Trust, and Transparency

I BELIEVE WHOLEHEARTEDLY that, for any relationship to strive, there has to be a basis of clarity and understanding. While we understand that no two persons are alike, we struggle with accepting people for whom they show us they truly are. I suspect that I have experienced hurt throughout many relationships (between friends, family, and significant others) because my expectations for said relationships were built on the premise that they were always going to be good to me. I held them to a standard that wasn't realistic.

After feeling pieces of my heart disintegrate every time a relationship didn't go as planned, I'd become callous and brutal with my words and my thoughts. I was convinced that being "real" and true to myself would ease my pain, and it would allow people to see that I was a force to be reckoned with. People who brought negativity were going to fall away, and everything would be right in the world.

The main issue with that is that friends and family don't just walk away. A conscious effort has to be made to kill these relationships. So, I came up with a strategy to determine which relationships were valuable enough to hold on to, and which ones needed to be fixed or eliminated. It made no sense that I would get frazzled or hurt when things didn't turn out the way I hoped. Please don't misconstrue this as me being bitter over things not going my way. There are just some relationships that need special attention. They drain you mentally, physically, and emotionally, and they prohibit you from being the best you, you can be.

In an attempt to live a more peaceful and less stressful life, let me introduce you to the 3 T's: Truth, Trust, and Transparency.

Being truthful in any relationship is one of the most fundamental ways to ensure relationships work. We've all seen that movie where someone withholds, or embellishes, relevant information from a friend and, when the friend finds out, the friendship is damaged, and often ruined, forever. Being truthful solidifies a blossoming bond and strengthens an existing friendship. With this in place, it breeds trust.

Transparency, to me, is honesty that is given freely. Being able to speak up about situations without being asked, shows a party's willingness and openness to protect and grow the relationship.

I didn't see the 3T's in my family, not at the same time at least. I believe that if my parents were able to exhibit these signs, they would have saved both themselves and their children from a lot of hurt and heartache.

It's the same with my relationship with God. I rebelled hard against the plan He had in store for me. I didn't trust God, nor did I love Him. It was hard to trust when believing in Him became questionable. How could there be truth hidden in so much uncertainty? After attempting suicide on more than one occasion, I thought that God wasn't who I needed Him to be.

I remember the first time I tried to take my life. It was shortly after my father beat me for that pornographic magazine. I didn't know what to do with my life after that incident. I was no longer "needed" by my peers, and I slipped back into invisibility. I had no purpose, and therefore no reason to live. I thought that I was just a nuisance to my parents. I was an embarrassment to my father, and my mother found joy in gossiping about me to her friends. I had no one in my corner, and I had nothing to lose.

Back then, the concept of suicide with children wasn't as prevalent as it is today, but somehow at the time, it seemed like the right thing to do. Right around that time, I was learning in science class about the heart and how it functioned in the body. I learned about the blood vessels, veins, and arteries, and how they all came together to circulate blood around the body. My teacher went into great lengths about what could happen if any of these essential vessels were damaged.

I used that knowledge to carry out my plan. I arrived home early one evening, and found a razor blade that I believed was my fathers. I intended to cut my wrists, bleed out in the middle of the living room floor, and greet my parents with my lifeless, cold body when they arrived at home. I was struggling with my self worth and at this point, everything started weighing on me. I wrote a long letter and left it on the dining room table. The letter said something along these lines of:

Dear Mommy and Daddy,
I tried to be everything that you wanted me to be, but I
can't. I go to church because you say I have to go. I go

to school because you say I have to go. It is clear that there is nothing that I can do right. My feelings mean nothing to you. I feel like you don't love me because you don't understand me and, for that, I'm sorry. I don't know how to change. I can't understand why we don't have the bond like the other children with their parents. I want to look like the other girls, with their long, straight hair and neither of you will make me straighten my hair or tell me why. Why do you hate me so much? Daddy likes all the girls with the long straight hair, and the ones who wear the pants (I wasn't allowed to wear pants), but you both make me walk around looking ugly. I finally made friends at school and now they make fun of me when they see the light blood stains printing through my shirt. They know what you did to me. Don't worry. I wont be a burden anymore. I'll make it easier for everybody and just disappear. It's not like you're going to miss me anyway.

Bye.

As I think back, my reasons for wanting to take my life were superficial. Yes, I was bullied in school, and I couldn't hang out with the "cool" kids, but that wasn't the motivation I used to try to end my life. I wanted to end my life because I couldn't get my parents to understand my needs. I was like an inanimate object to them, sometimes treated as though I had no feelings. I didn't have a problem with my parents saying no to the things I wanted. I had a problem with the reasoning behind it all. Maybe in their eyes, they thought that the things that I craved would breed rebellion. In my eyes, it would make me fit in, and feel less like the class target.

I think it's important to communicate with our children, even if what they believe doesn't line up with our beliefs. Something as simple as my hair, caused me to be ostracized by many of my classmates, and it could have all been corrected if my parents took the time to see that I struggled with low self-esteem. I'm not saying they should have allowed me to get my hair relaxed, but I'm sure they could have found ways to build my self-confidence and self-love.

I sat on the living room floor, blade in hand, and waited for the show on COURT TV to end. Then it was time. I slowly cut my left wrist and immediately shrieked in pain. I had no idea that slashing my wrists would be so painful. There was nearly no blood at all. If I was going to do it, I had to do it quickly. I tried slashing my right wrist, but the pain I experienced immediately had me second guessing suicide altogether.

My plans to leave a bloody mess failed, and I

didn't have a backup plan.

I could run away.
I could run in the street and get hit by a car.

I had no choice but to give up. I threw the blade in the garbage can outside, tore the letter into pieces and discarded it at school the next day.

The second time I tried to kill myself, I was 19. I didn't know how I wanted to do it, but I needed to go. My life was crap. Nothing ever worked in my favor and, this time, I knew for a fact my parents hated me. This was right after the fight I had with my father over the iPhone. He only wanted me around for the things I could do for him. My mother didn't want me living with her, and it was the confirmation that I needed from all those years of neglect and unlovingness.

I wanted to jump off the roof of a building, or off of a bridge. I did not want to be found. I just wanted to be a distant memory.

When I moved in with Harriet, I secluded myself from everyone, and went nowhere. I was locked up in my room for weeks watching Love and Basketball on my laptop and occasionally eating. That movie unconsciously gave me hope that regardless of the situations I'd faced, there would always be one person who would understand and love me, despite my faults – God.

But once again, I couldn't go through with taking my life. Something deep down on the inside was telling me otherwise. I knew there was something special about me. I didn't know what it was or whom it came from. I just knew that there had to be more to life than living unhappily. So, I began to search. And for years, I searched and made many mistakes, all in an attempt to figure out who I was and what I needed to do to live a fulfilled life.

In the end, I learned that nothing in life was going to be perfect and things weren't always going to go as planned, but as long as I had a relationship with Him that was built on truth, trust, and transparency, He'd be right by my side. I was now on my new journey to mastering peace.

CHAPTER 14

Master Peace

PEACE—THE ABSENCE of turmoil. Freedom from disturbance. Tranquility at its finest. Can one truly master peace? My life has been filled with ups, downs, rebellion, hate, neglect, triumph, growth, and love.

For many years, I struggled with identifying the root of most, if not all, of my problems. I blamed other people and didn't take responsibility for my actions. I became careless with my words and deeds, and finally, I hit rock bottom and was able to look at the life decisions that I'd made. I had to work hard to correct them.

In total transparency, I knew that I had a long

way to go. To truly master peace, I knew that I needed to forgive. For many years, I'd hear pastors preach about forgiveness and not truly understand what the concept meant. I would forgive with my mouth, but my heart was still filled with bitterness, resentment, hurt, pain, and hate. Forgiveness is supposed to bring peace, and I couldn't seem to grasp that.

I believed within my heart that I had forgiven my father. I'd say it out loud to prove to people that I had no hard feelings towards him, but it was all a lie. Deep on the inside, he still ignited ugly emotions that only stole pieces of me. I couldn't understand why I couldn't genuinely forgive him. Then it hit me. Someone once said to me that forgiveness wasn't for the person who wronged me; it was for me. I couldn't forgive because I was busy holding on to the things he did and the apologies he didn't make, and I allowed my fickle feelings to dictate how to deal with him.

I wanted to dwell in true forgiveness, so I began taking baby steps towards a peaceful life by slowly making amends. That meant that I had to get out of my comfort zone and address issues that tormented my childhood and transition into adulthood. The goal was to be open to change on both ends, so we could rebuild and start fresh. This was difficult because my pride prevented me from wanting anything to do with my father. I forced myself to be as objective as I could because, deep down, I wanted to stop wasting time and move on.

My brother and I decided to meet with my father in October of 2017 in a bustling food court in a mall on Long Island. That month marked a little over eight years since the cell phone incident when I moved out of his apartment. This would mark the first time in years since we sat down to talk and, the truth is, I didn't know what to expect. I didn't know if he was going to be receptive of what I had to say. I wanted closure, not another argument. We needed to address the most critical factors that contributed to our dysfunction.

We spoke for a while before he realized that both myself and my brother were now adults and that his authoritative persona was no longer a threat or scare tactic to either of us. My brother and I was not willing to back down from his ignorance; instead, we tackled each situation head-on, in an attempt to fix our broken bond.

I spoke to him about some of the things that I did growing up, like stealing from him. Many years ago, my father worked for one of Jamaica's biggest phone companies, and at that time, the company dominated the new wireless market. To make phone calls, or send text messages, the phones would have to be preloaded with money from calling cards. Back then, calling cards were not electronic but were in the form of physical cards that came preloaded with anything between $50JMD to $1000JMD.

After the beat-down that he gave me for the pornographic magazine, and the suicidal attempt, I felt that I should make him hurt just as much as I did. I would take his phone cards, bring them to school, and pass them out like they were valueless. In the end, this only hurt my family. I wasn't smart enough to understand that then.

It was hard being a young Christian, but even harder when the example set in front of me made me question what to truly believe.

I went on to talk about the Christian values he wanted my brother and I to live up to, but struggled to abide by himself. When asked why, he had no rebuttal. It was hard being a young Christian, but even harder when the example set in front of me made me question what to truly believe.

I discussed how severely he beat me for that pornographic magazine and questioned why he didn't check in to see the reason I had even resorted to viewing such lewd entertainment. He had no valid response.

My brother and I brought to his attention the indecent conversations we had both overheard him partake in, both here in the States and back home in Jamaica. He was a little surprised when I bluntly repeated some of the explicit things I heard him say, then he blatantly denied that it ever happened.

I brought up how he dealt with me the night before I moved to college - how he attacked me and resorted to name calling and esteem bashing based on heresy he received from the habitual liar, Paul. I was angry that he was so quick to believe the words of a young man who had absolutely no credibility.

"No man ever wants to hear about their daughter being portrayed in that light", my father confessed.

As much as that may have been true, I challenged him, suggesting he should have forced Paul to present him with facts before jumping the gun. I explained that that altercation drove a colossal wedge between us, which admittedly was the icing on the cake for me. Even at that moment of transparency and emotion, he never once asked me if any of it was true, which forced me to believe that he already had his preconceived ideas about it.

Why believe the truth when the lie is more entertaining?

That was one of the things that hurt me the most, and he could not even muster up the courage to apologize for jumping to conclusions.

We sat and spoke with my father for a little over 2 hours and accomplished absolutely nothing. He was still unwilling to see the error of his ways but wanted to sit down with us again soon. I had an issue with that. My father has always been known to sweep his problems under the rug and act as though nothing happened.

Why believe the truth when the lie is more entertaining?

I can't live like that.

It was and still is, hard for me to pretend like everything is good when it isn't.

Why couldn't he admit how wrong he was?

The inner child in me was screaming out for closure, and he just wouldn't give it. My brother and I both knew that he realized the error of his ways based on the weak answers he gave us.

But why be so prideful now?

You're in a position where you may lose your children forever, and you're still prideful?

Enough was enough. That dysfunctional cycle was ending with me.

You don't have to rebuild a relationship with everyone you've forgiven. Just because you're at peace doesn't mean that they aren't still toxic.

My peace was a priority. I needed to be able to protect my mental, emotional and spiritual health. I decided - in a split second - that I couldn't wait for an apology to claim my peace. I was dependent on my father to do right by me, to secure my happiness, but the truth was that I was holding hostage my joy and peace of mind. It was time to take it back.

I cannot stay bitter because he won't apologize.

That day, I forgave my father and I washed my hands clean of every bad and hurtful thing that my father ever said and did to me, and I walked away - free, with no intentions of looking back. I learned that you don't have to rebuild a relationship with everyone you've forgiven. Just because you're at peace doesn't mean that they aren't still toxic.

My father will always be my father, and I will always be his daughter, but dysfunction and toxicity are where I draw the line in any relationship. Hurt people hurt people, and I was tired of hurting people, so I disconnected myself from my primary source of hurt, and have been living a more purposeful life.

I pray for my father often. I feel that this may be the only resource left that may work. I remember calling him some time after our meeting, telling him about some not so pleasant dreams that I had about him, with the intent of motivating him to get himself together, but nothing changed. The zeal to reinvent himself was not there, but the excuses about all the great things he did for our family all those years ago in Jamaica resurfaced. That was his guilt trap, and I was not going to fall for it - again.

Today, the relationship I have with my mother is better than what it was years ago. She and I may not see eye to eye on everything, but we have developed a bond in which we can talk. It's still not 100% what I'd like it to be, but I can live with that.

Altogether, I believe that my parents' sole purpose was to introduce me to God. God has always been there and told us that He will never leave us nor forsake us. Share with Him your dreams and fears, and He will direct your path.

At the age of 19, I went through a rebirth and a transition. I was able to live and interact with other families, and I realized that blood doesn't make us family. Flesh and blood don't mean that you will have the loving and caring relationship that you want. Mastering peace, for you, may take you down a more traditional route, but for me, it was the opposite.

Putting God in the center of everything that you do can help you grasp that peace that has been missing from your life for so long. I noticed that the moments when I wasn't closest to Him were the times when things became so much more difficult. I have given all my burdens to Him, and I have no intentions of taking them back. God will never give us more than we can bear; however, when things become harder than usual, He will never turn us away or leave us stranded. God has bailed me out of every difficult situation I've ever been in, often before I even realize. He granted me the desires of my heart, once I surrendered to His will and allowed Him to be the God of my life.

Many of my experiences were inevitable; however, my church family didn't play enough of a vital role in my life.

My message to my church family is simple.

Learn to love. There is more to people than what you see on Sunday mornings. You really don't know how much your kind words, good deeds and gestures, and genuine love will impact someone going through hard times. Genuinely treat people the way you'd want to be treated. Embrace them for who they are, love them without recourse, and watch how that person's life will turn around. God gave us all free will. Don't disregard someone or their feelings because their choice isn't necessarily what you would have chosen. Love people, regardless of their lifestyle. Again, you don't have to agree with it, but that doesn't mean your love should stop.

Pastors and ministers, you have been called to be a beacon of light for your congregation and the world. We look up to you, trust in you, and in many cases, hang on to your every word. Make time for your congregation. Families should be able to reach out for support from you in their marriages, with their children, and even for themselves. They should not only see and hear from you when you have a "word" for them.

Parents, there is no way you can do everything on your own. It is ok to ask for help or to admit that you don't know how to solve a problem, instead of creating a cycle of dysfunction for your children to continue.

They look up to you and love you wholeheartedly, and a day will come when they will remember all the things that you have done to and for them, and they will hold you accountable for your actions, whether good or bad. Teach your children to strive for their dreams and encourage them to learn from your mistakes so that they can be better versions of you.

My friends, don't ever allow anyone to dictate or determine how your life should be. Never entertain the negativity that comes from people who only pretend to have your best interest at heart. Whenever you are told that you won't amount to anything, or that you will never be better than your mother or father, or that you'll only be good at laying on your back, do not feed into that garbage. It is a lie! You are strong, ambitious, and can do anything you put your mind to. Remove yourself from people who can't see that fire, that zeal, that passion in you. Don't make rash decisions based on emotions that may change. Be smart, be vigilant. Even though life and death are in the power of the tongue, you have the power to rebuke anything that is said to you that is not of God.

If they tell you that you are too old to go back to school, push back.
If they tell you that the business you want to start won't

work, push back.

If they tell you that you're living a life destined for failure, push back.

Stop sharing your thoughts and dreams with just anyone. Not everyone wants to see your success; many rejoice in your shortcomings. Work in silence, and don't make any announcements until all your work is done.

I've learned many lessons throughout my life, and I know that there are many more that I'll have to face. No longer will I allow a future filled with uncertainty to cripple me with fear and disable me from being my best self. If I had allowed fear and anxiety to control me, this book would have never been written. If I had listened to the person who told me that running a publishing company would be too difficult, I would have given up. Someone once said that it would be best if you didn't allow the mistakes you made to have any of your energy, time or space. You can do and be anything that you put your mind to. Find your purpose. Walk in it, and before you know it, you'll be on your journey to Master Peace.

LIFE

CHAPTER 15

The Spiritual Perception of My Life

I WAS FREE. The feeling of independence felt sweet. I had just rented my first apartment, and I was thrilled. It was a beautiful studio that had subsections for a little kitchen and a nook. It was big enough for me to have a section for my bedroom and a "chill" section for whenever my friends came over.

It was painted in full white and was absolutely spotless. The windows were positioned perfectly, allowing the radiance of the sun to penetrate all four walls. There was just a heavenly glow in the room, and I promised myself that I would maintain this space. I didn't want to lose my apartment.

After living there for a couple of months, I started to slack off a little bit. The walls that were once white begun to look a little off-white. You could hardly distinguish the "chill" section from the bedroom and the dining area. It was either the sun was no longer as radiant as it used to be, or the windows weren't as transparent. My walls became dull, and the reflection of the sunlight was completely different.

The friends that I would always invite over soon started to change because I was changing. They would come over often and not respect my home because I didn't respect it myself. Before long, my friends would bring their friends over—people whom I would never usually hang out with, much less invite into my sanctuary.

One morning, I heard a knock at my door, thinking it was just one of my friends. I told the person,

"Come in. The door is open," and in walked this tall, handsome man.

He was dark, with curly hair and perfect cheekbones. His smile was luminous, with pristine white teeth, but more than anything, he had the deepest dimples that could change the temperature in any room. The way he carried himself was amazing. Physically, he was perfect. He seemed to be everything that I've ever wanted in a man. He stole my breath.

I was thinking to myself that this had to be my gift from God. Whoever he was, he had to be the one! He looked familiar, but I couldn't quite figure out where I knew him from. He claimed he was an old friend who came to get reacquainted. Nothing he was saying sounded familiar to me. Then he started telling me about all the things that I did in church. He pointed out which solo I sang in the choir and which Sunday School class I taught.

I still couldn't figure out who he was. He started saying that all those things didn't matter anymore, because I had all that I needed right here, in my little room. An uneasy spirit came over me. He then boldly stated that this was all that life had to offer me. All that was left for me to do was to continue to live carefree, and my life would be complete!

Sudden panic and fear gripped me. I quickly asked him to leave. He said no. I sternly asked him to reveal himself to me because somehow, I didn't think he was whom he said he was. He smiled and said he was my friend.

He told me to stop worrying about his identity. He believed that it didn't matter who he was anymore; he just knew that we were meant to be together. He said we shared similar characteristics.

"What characteristics?" I asked.

He said I wasn't clean or honest. I was proud, boastful, and respected no one. I was selfish, and living a selfless life seemed impossible. He told me I was lucky to have someone to love me unconditionally, and I disposed of that love, to get the microwave love; love that got real hot fast and died at the speed of life. He said,

"Did you forget that you were the temple of God and that the spirit of God lived in you? Seeing that you already defiled your temple by allowing me in, God will destroy you".

Now I knew exactly who he was, and again, I asked him to leave, and again he said he wasn't going anywhere. He believed that because I allowed him to come into my home, he would be living there permanently – rent-free. He wanted to feed off what strength I had left. He made it crystal clear that nothing or no one could get him out. He was stuck to me like sand on my skin. What he didn't realize was that although brushing it off wouldn't completely get rid of the sand, a nice shower would make me clean.

I called on the name of Jesus, and he laughed.

He said that I gave up my opportunity to call on

the Lord's name. It was too late. The Lord had already left when the walls of my heart changed from white to off white. I screamed the name of the Lord again, and he said,

"God can't work in confusion, and your heart is messy and unorganized."

This time I yelled the name of Jesus, and he said,

"You can't get rid of me without fasting and prayer, and that's something I know you can't do because your flesh is your weakness. Your flesh can't battle with my spirit."

This being that came into my house, and became a squatter, was no longer attractive. He transformed into a hideous beast. He resembled nothing nearly close to the image of God. So, I did what I was taught years before; I tried the spirit.

"In the name of Jesus, reveal yourself!", I screamed.

He confessed to being the adversary who came as an angel of light to steal from me, kill me, and destroy me.

You see, the walls of my apartment represented my heart; spotless and without blemish when I had just accepted the Lord in my life. For months, things seemed to flow smoothly. The light shining in through the windows represented the glory of God shining in my life. The sections in the room represented the order and principle in my life. Everything was line upon line, precept upon precept.

But somewhere along the line, I became comfortable. I let my guard down and, slowly, minor instances became major bad habits. I would forget to pray one night before bed and, before I knew it, I had stopped praying altogether, telling myself that I prayed recently and that should maintain me, not remembering that I was nothing but a broken vessel that needed to be consistently filled, for my anointing was continuously flowing through the cracks. I didn't realize that a prayer a day kept the devil away. A prayer a day kept my vessel filled. I stopped fasting, which was just telling the devil to come in.

The friends in my life represented all the fruits and gifts of the spirit. Love was the one that gave me that feeling of hope. She gave me that strength to move on. She made me feel safe. Peace made me calm, and she killed all the anger that would try to break me down. Faithfulness was the one who made me believe that after every downfall came something greater. Joy was my best friend. We never went anywhere on our own. We were inseparable.

Joy was always in my home until I pushed her out. Goodness, Kindness, and Gentleness were sweethearts. The twins, Patience, and Self-Control helped to keep me in check those times I thought I was going to lose my cool. You see, I traded my friends, for those "so-called friends" - the friends that pleased my flesh. Anything that made me feel good; I did it. And that's when the walls of my heart started to change.

What was happening to me?

My strength was fading. I tried to run away but could hardly move.

Was this the end for me?
What was I left to do?

Just as Sampson beckoned strength to destroy the walls of the Philistine Temple, I mustered the strength and screamed the name of Jesus with what was left inside my already drained body. And instantly, like a rushing mighty wind, the Lord dispatched His angels, and like a powerful force, they marched together, linked by the arms, towards this creature of destruction.

The deceiver's back was against the wall. He had

nowhere to turn. He saw an exit and ran. On his way out, he yelled at me saying,

"This isn't the last of me. I know you better than you know yourself and that means you're gonna have a crack in your heart again, and I'm gonna break you down when I get back."

Instantly, the voice of the Lord, loud like a trumpet, said to me,

"Repent and abstain from the things of this flesh and the adversary won't have room to move in. My child, the ways of the Lord are just. I will take control of your life. I will make you whole. I will be your love. I will keep you. I will make you happy because I am your God."

Written By:
Melissa T. Walker
12/03/2011

ACKNOWLEDGEMENTS

First and foremost, I'd like to thank God for providing an avenue for me to express myself wholeheartedly. He has proven time and time again that He has always – and will always – have my back.

I want to thank my therapist for encouraging me to put pen to paper and to bring to light the things that have consumed me for years. Without that help, I would not have changed.

To my husband who gently pushed me when I wanted to give up, thank you. To all my family members and friends who showed genuine concern for my stability and mental health, thank you.

Finally, for everyone who read the pages of this book, thank you for your support.

ABOUT THE AUTHOR

Melissa T. Walker is an author, motivational speaker, and a newlywed marriage coach who believes in educating women through coaching, books, blogs that encourages growth, change, love, peace, and hope.

At a young age, she realized that dysfunctional relationships had a severe impact on the mental, physical, and emotional well-being of anyone it encountered.

Melissa started her journey helping women in 2015 and today, her primary function is encourage women to be the best versions of themselves.

Melissa earned and a bachelor's degree in Business Management & Finance from Brooklyn College in New York, and a master's degree in Human Resources Management from Nova Southeastern University in Ft. Lauderdale, Florida. She is currently obtaining her masters in Marriage & Family Therapy from Northcentral University.